CULTURES OF AMERICA

MEXICAN AMERICANS

By Petra Press

Marshall Cavendish
New York • London • Toronto

Published by
Marshall Cavendish Corporation
2415 Jerusalem Avenue
P.0. Box 587
North Bellmore, New York 11710, U.S.A.

Developed, edited, and designed by Water Buffalo Books, Milwaukee

Project director: Mark Sachner
Art director: Sabine Beaupré
Picture researcher: Diane Laska
Editorial: Valerie Weber and Eileen Foran
Cover Design: Lee Goldstein
Marshall Cavendish development editor: MaryLee Knowlton
Marshall Cavendish editorial director: Evelyn Fazio

Picture Credits: Sabine Beaupré 1994: 7, 19; © The Bettmann Archive: 6, 15, 20; © Geopress/H. Armstrong Roberts: 14; © Gierth/Mauritius/H. Armstrong Roberts: 8; © Jane Gleeson: 56; © Hazel Hankin: 13; © Bonnie Kamin: 74; © R. Krubner/H. Armstrong Roberts: 10, 12; © Antonio Pérez: 4, 30, 33, 34, 62; © Antonio Pérez/¡Exito!: Cover, 1, 28, 31, 35, 37, 38, 40, 44, 47 (bottom), 52, 54, 66, 68, 69, 73; © Paul M. Perez: 36, 60, 72; © David C. Phillips: 51; © Kelly A. Shannon: 5, 16, 39, 42, 43, 45, 47 (top), 59, 61; © A. Tovy/H. Armstrong Roberts: 17; © UPI/Bettmann: 18, 22, 24, 27, 75

Library of Congress Cataloging-in-Publication Data

Press, Petra.
    Mexican Americans / Petra Press.
        p.   cm. — (Cultures of America)
    Includes bibliographical references and index.
    ISBN 0-7614-0150-4 (set) : ISBN 0-7614-0152-0 (Mexican Americans)
    1. Mexican Americans--Juvenile literature. [1. Mexican Americans.] I. Title II. Series.
E184.M5P74   1995
973'.046872--dc20   94-48112
                                                          CIP
                                                          AC

To PS – MS

Printed and bound in the U.S.A.

CONTENTS

INTRODUCTION

Of all the stories Americans have to tell, none are more exciting, more dramatic, or more magical than those Mexican Americans tell about their immigrant ancestors. Almost every aspect of Mexican American culture — food, art, dress, music, religion, architecture, farming methods, and courtship rituals — can trace its origins to Spanish and American Indian influences that go back five hundred years or more. Unlike most ethnic groups who came to the U.S. by choice, the first Mexicans to become Americans didn't migrate at all; it was the U.S.-Mexican boundary that moved and that changed their nationalities along with it.

Even the later groups of Mexicans who did immigrate to the U.S. in the nineteenth and twentieth centuries differed in an important way from other American immigrants: They did not readily give up their language, religion, and other cultural traditions to assimilate into the great Anglo "melting pot," in spite of tremendous pressures to do so. Yet even as they struggled hard to overcome prejudice, economic inequality, and discrimination (a fight that continues in many areas even today), they never stopped enriching American culture with their celebration of life. Their tremendous contributions have expanded every facet of American life — from art and music to sports, architecture, and, of course, cuisine.

A young girl accompanies her mother, who works as a flower vendor at the Floating Gardens of Xochomilco in central Mexico. The exotic, tropical flowers are a favorite with residents and visitors alike.

CHAPTER ONE

LEAVING A HOMELAND
LIFE IN OLD MEXICO

Miguel Reyes was making the long journey back to his village from Guadalajara on foot because his family was too poor to own a horse or burro. The weariness he felt was not so much from the miles he had covered the last few days, but from having to return to his wife and children empty-handed — again. Work was scarce even in a big city like Guadalajara in 1841.

As he walked along the well-rutted path, Miguel's thoughts drifted to memories of his brother Juan who had fought — and died — so bravely in the great fight for independence twenty years earlier. They were going to change the world back then. They were going to rip the land away from the greedy Spanish landowners and divide it up among the starving peasant families to whom it really belonged. He laughed a sad laugh at the memory. Here it was, twenty years later, and the new government still hadn't figured out how to divide up the land. He and his neighbors were poorer now than they'd ever been. But as the sun started to set behind the hills, Miguel shook off these troubling thoughts and focused instead on his daughter's upcoming confirmation, a joyous event the whole village would celebrate. He was only a few short hours from home and could almost smell the delicious chicken *mole* (pronounced moh-LAY) his wife would be cooking for his return. He smiled and quickened his pace.

Miguel was not the only one to be worried about his family in the mid-1800s. Most Mexicans were poor and, in spite of the industrial revolution that was changing lives in the cities of Europe and the United States, still lived in the same hard conditions as their great-great-grandfathers had. Many of Miguel's neighbors were packing up and moving north to the California territory in hopes of finding work. But being poor in Mexico did not mean living a bleak or dull existence. Even if times were so bad that they didn't have enough to eat, Mexican peasants still surrounded themselves with beautiful things, like their vibrant, handwoven clothing and hand-painted pots and bowls. And even those who barely had enough corn to eat for months at a time had their faith, strong families, and close community ties to make their lives rich and meaningful.

Because the U.S. Southwest was once part of Mexico, the first Mexican Americans did not have to emigrate.

A GUIDE TO PRONUNCIATION

Spanish vowel	English sound
a	ah
e	ay
i	ee
o	oh
u	oo
y	ee

Examples	Pronunciation
Acapulco	Ah — kah — POOL — koh
Aztec	AHS — tehk
Hernán Cortés	Ehr — NAHN Kor — TESS
Guadalajara	Hwah — dah — lah — HAR — rah
Hacienda	ah — see — EHN — dah
Benito Juárez	Beh — NEE — toh HWAH — ress
México	MEH — hee — koh
Moctezuma	Mohk — teh — SOO — mah

A Rich Mixture of Spanish and Indian Cultures

Almost every part of Mexican culture — food, music, art, religion, dress, architecture, farming, even courtship rituals — has traces of both Native and Spanish influence. In fact, by the 1800s, most people in Mexico claimed both American Indian and Spanish ancestors. During the three hundred years Spain occupied Mexico, from the mid-1500s to the early 1800s, their relationship with local Native cultures was one of violence, exploitation, and harsh politi-

The ruins of an old Spanish church are a dramatic presence in Mitla, a small town in southern Mexico. Spanish monks built their churches with thick, windowless adobe walls that would provide the protection of a strong fort.

THE INDIANS: ALWAYS ON THE BOTTOM OF THE LADDER

During the colonial period, the Spanish imposed the idea that social status depended not on one's wealth or level of education, but on one's descent. Spaniards born in Spain, they reasoned, were the most superior, followed by Spaniards born in the Mexican colonies. Then came *mestizos* (children of mixed Spanish-Indian marriages). Further down the social ladder were *mulattos* (Mexicans of Spanish-African ancestry), *zambos* (those of Indian-African ancestry), and *chinos* (those with Spanish-Asian or Indian-Asian ancestry). Pure-blood Indians, whatever their culture (and it is estimated that there were about fifty-five separate Native societies in Mexico) were considered — by far — the most inferior. Sadly, after Mexico gained its independence in 1821, official government policies continued to maintain that Indians were inferior to other Mexicans and were not entitled to equal rights.

cal control. In spite of their contempt for the Indians, however, more and more Spanish intermarried with local Indians over the centuries until few people were left who could claim to be either pure Spanish or pure Indian. The descendants of these marriages created a new ethnic group called *mestizo.*

Making a Living in a Poor Rural Society

In the 1800s and early 1900s, Mexico was still primarily an agricultural country, and while some people lived and worked in cities like Guadalajara or Mexico City, most lived in rural communities and worked as farmers. A few of the landowning peasants (less than 10 percent) were lucky enough to own property in fertile areas and could raise livestock and grow moneymaking crops such as sugar cane, coffee, bananas, and grains. At busy times of the year, they even hired other, poorer peasants to help with the extra work. Poorer farmers worked land that could only grow corn and squash, often renting the land they farmed instead of owning it. The poorest who couldn't even afford to rent simply took over small plots of land on mountainsides and in other barren areas that no one else wanted.

Most farmers existed on a diet made up primarily of *maize,* or corn. They had hundreds of ways of cooking it, and in harder years, it often meant the only thing between their families and starvation. While each farmer earned his income by farming, just about every peasant also worked his own *milpa,* or corn field, to feed his family.

Raising corn took a lot of time and hard work. First the field had to be tilled with a wooden plow, which was pulled by oxen if the owner could afford them and by the owner himself if he couldn't. Most peasants still used the same old-fashioned planting sticks, or *coas,* that the Spanish had introduced to Mexico three hundred years earlier. A man would walk down a row, first using the wider end of the stick to brush the soil, and then using the sharper end to poke a hole for the seed. His wife would follow him down the rows with a bag of seeds, dropping them into the holes and then using her feet to fill the holes up with dirt.

Harvesting the corn was even harder. Men and women both worked the fields with

Named Papanoa, this small fishing village lies along the Pacific coastline of southern Mexico. Thatched palms, which provide both shade and ventilation, have long served as the perfect roofing material for houses in this tropical climate.

baskets strapped to their backs and small sharp lances called *pizcadors* attached to their third fingers that made it easier to cut the corn husks from the stalks. In the time between planting and harvesting, both men and women pulled weeds and prayed for a fruitful harvest.

Life in a Mexican Village

In the nineteenth century, whether a peasant was a farmer or a blacksmith or a merchant, his community was one of the cornerstones of his family's life. People lived in communities ranging in size from a few families to hundreds and even thousands. The smallest places were the *rancherías* or *parajes* (both words mean "small settlement"); the

larger were the *pueblos* (villages) and *ciudades* (cities). The names of Mexico's pueblos and ciudades were often unusual and even poetic, like *Mixcoac*, "The Snake of Clouds," and *Texcoztingo*, which means "Laughing Hills." Others were named after Catholic saints or Mexican heroes, while some had names given to them by early Spanish invaders.

A pueblo, or village, was usually a group of simple houses clustered around a fine church. People came into these villages from surrounding rancherías to trade food and crafts in the local marketplace and to celebrate religious *fiestas,* or celebrations. These villages also housed schools, chapels, municipal buildings, and public fountains.

Perhaps the most important part of the pueblo, however, was the central plaza, or the *zócolo,* where people gathered to attend band concerts and to meet, talk, and gossip with their neighbors. It was also one of the only opportunities Mexican teenagers had to interact with the opposite sex. One or more nights a week (depending on local custom) there would be a promenade in which the young people would dance around the plaza to band music. They were not allowed to dance together — only to circle in opposite directions, but it did give them a chance to flirt.

Because most of the people living in and around the pueblos were very poor, their houses were simple, inexpensive, and perfectly adapted to their environment. The materials and techniques used to construct them changed very little from pre-Spanish times. Most were made of logs (where wood was available) or adobe bricks and had

BLESSING A HOUSE IN YALALAG, OAXACA

To protect a new house and its inhabitants from harm by witchcraft, the head of the family placed small pine crosses at the four corners of the foundation, each of which was sprinkled with the blood of freshly beheaded chickens. (The resinous pine of the crosses also acted as a defense against lightning.) All of the wood used to build the house was cut on the night of a full moon.

thatched roofs of palm leaves or grass. In some areas, tile roofs were more common, but almost all the houses, no matter how humble, were decorated with potted plants and flowers. Floors were usually made of dried mud, with the surrounding fences made of piled stone or live cactus. It was the custom for

THE BARE NECESSITIES

Most households were only furnished with the barest necessities: something to cook on and in, something to eat from, and something to sleep on. The cooking hearth was usually nothing more than a flat clay griddle supported by three stones over a fire. Kitchen utensils were clay pots (*ollas*), pottery bowls, and mugs for serving the food, with hollowed out gourds to hold liquids. People used their fingers or bits of *tortillas* (corn pancakes) instead of knives, forks, and spoons. Every household also had a *metate,* a three-legged stone with a long roller for grinding corn, a *molcajete* (mortar and pestle) for mashing chilies and tomatoes, and at least one *machete* , a long curved or straight steel knife.

A *petate,* or reed mat spread on the ground, took the place of chairs during the day and served as a bed at night. In places like the tropics, where it was dangerous to sleep on the ground because of snakes and scorpions, people slept in hammocks. Occasionally, in more prosperous households, there were a few low stools or benches. (The more well-to-do, of course, could afford tables, chairs, beds, china dishes, and more modern utensils.)

However poor the furnishings, every house had a household altar. A small table was built to hold the oil paintings of the family's patron saints, vases of bright fresh flowers, incense burners, crosses, and candles.

Local residents shop in the vegetable market in Merida, on the Yucatan Peninsula, which juts out into the Gulf of Mexico. Villages have long tried to be as self-sufficient as possible, with families growing their own produce, making their own clothing, and trading with others.

every man to build his own house with the help of relatives and friends, whom he would then help in return. There was always a feast to commemorate the completed house and a special ceremony to drive away any evil spirits.

Houses could be round, square, or rectangular. Some were no more than one windowless room that served all the family's purposes. Sometimes a lean-to would be added to create a separate kitchen and a small pen to keep animals. Families who were a little better off would often build several unconnected, one-room buildings around a central patio, with separate quarters for sleeping, cooking, and working. These would also have such modern features as windows, roofed porches, and outhouses. The well-to-do families in the larger pueblos and cities (usually the landowners) would have elegant masonry houses instead of adobe, with long, grated windows and large, well-decorated patios.

Neighbors did far more than just help each other build homes. They were there for each other in times of joy and sorrow with help, gifts, and even money. Neighbors often borrowed items but always returned them again with a small gift of thanks. Children and young people were expected to greet their elders with great respect. Adults greeted each other warmly and inquired about the other's health and well-being. Most important of all, a promise made to a neighbor was always kept.

Making a Living in the Village

Village families tried to be as self-sufficient as possible by raising their own corn, beans, and squash and by weaving their own cloth for the family's clothes and blankets. What they couldn't make themselves, they got by bartering with their neighbors. In spite of these measures, there was still always a need for money, and villagers had a number of ways of earning it. Whatever work they did was usually seasonal, which meant that even highly skilled workers (like masons, carpenters, barbers, and shoemakers) had to find other jobs for at least part of the year. Many men hired out as farm laborers, leaving their villages for months at a time to work on plantations growing coffee, banana, or chicle (tree sap to be made into chewing gum). Some, like Miguel, looked for work in cities or traveled to far northern territories. Even so, the wages they earned were barely enough to help their families survive, let alone give them hope of ever rising out of poverty.

Family Life

As in many other cultures, the family has always been very important for Mexican

THE CUSTOM OF GIVING PILÒN

When people bought groceries or other items at a village store, it was customary for the store owner to give them a little present, like candy for the younger children, trinkets for the older ones, tobacco for the father, or a small household decoration for the mother. There was no law that said they had to do this, but those who didn't often found themselves without customers.

people. The basic family unit in the nineteenth and early twentieth centuries included not just parents and children, but other relatives such as grandparents or even a married son or daughter with spouse. In some villages, in central Mexico for example, it was customary for a new husband to live and work in his wife's father's house for the first year of their marriage in "payment" for the bride.

Mexican families have gone into many lines of work to make a living. These women help support their families by selling handicrafts on city streets. Many of these scarves, blankets, and table cloths are beautifully embroidered with Aztec or Mayan motifs handed down from their ancestors.

In a manner similar to that of their ancestors, Chamula Indians shop in a marketplace in Mexico's southernmost state of Chiapas. Traditional Indian clothing in Chiapas has long been inspired by the exotic tropical flowers that grow everywhere in this region, from the lush jungles to the thickly wooded mountains to the golden sands of its Pacific coastline.

Some fathers wanted their sons to continue to live with them after they were married to help in the fields or to carry on the father's trade.

While the father was considered the undisputed head of the family, the mother also had a great deal of authority. Mexican women did not necessarily lead sheltered lives without social rights, especially those of Indian descent. In addition to raising her children and running a household, a Mexican wife shared her husband's responsibilities—and even many of his pleasures. If he held a public or church office, for example, she would help him fulfill the obligations of his post. If he attended a neighborhood party or even visited a local tavern to gamble or socialize, she would often be there socializing with him. A man would not think of making important decisions without getting his wife's opinion — and consent — first.

Physical work has traditionally gone to Mexican men. This farmer in Baja California lives a hard life growing crops in a rocky desert climate.

It was traditionally the man's duty to handle the hard physical work like hunting, chopping wood, and plowing the fields, while it was the woman's job to take care of the children, wash, cook, sew, weave, embroider, haul water from the well or river, take care of the domestic animals, garden, and weed the corn fields. In reality, though, the woman often did a good part of the heavy work as well, especially when her husband needed help planting or harvesting.

Older people were not expected to work as hard as the young and middle-aged, but they were expected to contribute as best they could to the common welfare of their family and community.

Education

Although public rural schools did exist throughout Mexico in the mid-1800s, the great majority of children were educated at home. When their sons were eight, fathers began teaching them their occupations, while mothers began teaching their daughters the demanding tasks of running a household. A small percentage of children in rural areas

Unlike these children in rural Mexico, few children living in farming regions in the nineteenth and early twentieth centuries had the opportunity to attend school.

(both boys and girls) were encouraged to attend the small public schools, and some even left their villages for larger cities to obtain a higher education. But for the most part, villagers were suspicious of schools and the education they offered. They were afraid it would corrupt their children and encourage them to leave their villages for the temptations of the big cities, where they eventually would lead a life of sin and crime. It was also during these years in a child's life that he or she was taught to be self-supporting and to take an active part in the community. By the time children were fifteen or so, they were considered physically and socially mature enough for marriage.

Courtship and Marriage

In smaller, more traditional villages, young girls in their early and middle teens were not allowed to go out alone, even on household errands. Boys of the same age had a great deal more freedom, being allowed to go out and drink and have fun with older men in the village. They were not allowed to associate with girls, however. Girls usually got married at about fifteen and boys, seventeen. In most cases, the marriages were arranged by the parents, although many took their son's or daughter's wishes into consideration before arranging a match.

It was customary for the boy's parents (or sometimes a professional marriage-maker) to go to the home of the girl and "ask for the bride." Custom also demanded that this ritual take at least three or four visits and that at each visit, the girl's parents were to be given gifts, such as brandy, cigarettes, chocolate, bread, or fruit. Church weddings and the celebrations afterward differed in each village according to local custom, but for all it was a joyous and important event.

Mexican children grew up fast and had to face the harsh realities of raising their own families in desperate poverty. In the eighteenth and early nineteenth centuries, more and more young people went north to the United States (which they often called *El Norte*) looking for a way out. But the enduring faith that was so much a part of their daily lives, together with close family and community ties and the richness of their art, music, and culture, were strengths Mexicans carried with them wherever they traveled to survive. Those who overcame the hardships of making that journey north found that once they made it to the United States, they had more than poverty to overcome. They had to face discrimination, prejudice, persecution, and often even deportation back to the land they had just left.

LOVE WILL FIND A WAY

Just because teenage boys and girls were not allowed to talk to each other doesn't mean they didn't find ways of finding out if the one they admired loved them back. Sometimes a boy would wait for the girls to come out of church on Sundays and throw pebbles at their feet and watch for their reactions. Often a boy would find a way to get close to a girl just long enough to say hello to her — when she was returning from the village well with her family's water jar balanced on her head, for example, or when they passed each other during the plaza promenade. If she didn't ignore him, he knew he had won her heart.

This church in the town of Guanajuato was built by Spain in the fifteenth century. Their Catholic faith was one of the strengths that sustained Mexicans when they left their villages to head north.

Most Mexican immigrants with farming skills could find work in the U.S., but the pay was poor and the living conditions usually terrible. They were called migrant workers because they traveled from place to place throughout the Southwest, following the crops as they became ready for harvesting.

CHAPTER TWO

LIFE IN A NEW LAND
TO NUEVO MÉXICO AND *EL NORTE*

José Tarango waited all night on the plaza in Nayarit so he would be one of the first in line when the Americano showed up the next day to sign up new recruits. He was nervous because he knew there were many requirements he had to meet, and he worried that he might not be healthy enough to make the list. He'd heard the horror stories of the life *braceros* (the Mexican migrant farm workers) led in the United States — the long hours for low pay, the filthy living conditions, the contempt and prejudice of the Anglos — but he knew that for him it would be different.

He had also heard about the tremendous postwar prosperity Americans were enjoying. It was the 1950s, and business was booming. Practically every household had a big house, a new car, and one of those new televisions. José's dream was to make enough money so he and his wife, Angelita, could buy a nice house in an American suburb and send their children to fine American schools. He was young and strong and welcomed the chance to prove himself. As he stretched out on the hard bench, he rubbed the blisters on his sore hands with satisfaction. His friend Manuel

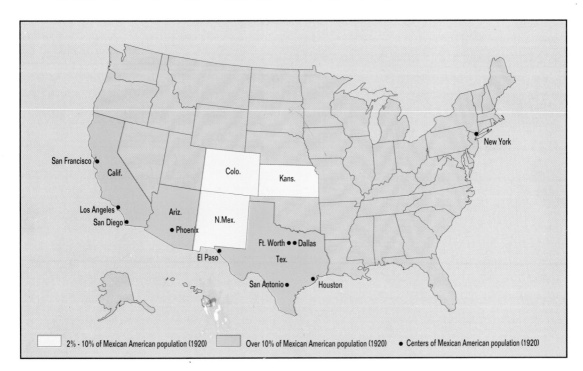

2% - 10% of Mexican American population (1920)   Over 10% of Mexican American population (1920)   • Centers of Mexican American population (1920)

In the years since the first annexation of Mexican land into the United States, Mexican Americans, their language, and their culture have extended their presence far beyond their origins in what is today the American Southwest.

Like settlers from the eastern U.S., many Mexican Americans built their first shelters out of blocks of sod, especially in areas where timber was scarce. Unlike the large estates, called *haciendas*, that wealthy landowners lived in, these houses could be leaky and uncomfortable, but they were better than sleeping out in the open. These settlers also used sod as fuel to heat their homes.

had told him that to pass the hand inspection — the test the recruiter used to determine if a man's hands were hard enough for farm work — he should work a shovel for two or three days until his palms were hard and blistered. He would pass. His bag was packed, and he had already said his good-byes. Aside from his clothes, Angelita had packed him enough fruit and tortillas to last him several days. He knew that if he was chosen, they would leave the same afternoon on the long bus ride to the U.S. border. He could hardly wait.

First Settlers of the U.S. Southwest

Unlike José, the first Mexican Americans did not have to immigrate to become U.S. citizens. There were Mexicans living in what is now the U.S. Southwest long before Anglo Americans got there. In the seventeenth, eighteenth, and early nineteenth centuries,

Mexicans and their Spanish rulers called this territory *Nuevo México*. The territory included what is now New Mexico, western and southern Texas, parts of California, Arizona, and Colorado, and the Mexican state of Chihuahua. Some Mexicans also settled as far north as Kansas and Nebraska.

Life in Nuevo México was based on the *hacienda* system. Haciendas were huge, privately owned estates carved out of land the Spanish nobles took from the local Pueblo Indians. Most of the semiarid land in these northern Spanish colonies was poorly suited to raising food crops but was ideal for raising cattle and sheep, so most of the haciendas were created to raise livestock (although there were also a few lumbering, mining, and farming haciendas). Settlers who migrated north from central Mexico to Nuevo México were *rancheros, peones*, or *vaqueros*. The wealthy rancheros (usually of Spanish descent) were the owners of the haciendas; the poor peones, or tenant farmers, worked the lands of the hacienda for the rancheros in exchange for small plots of their own; and the vaqueros were the cowhands who handled the livestock. There were also a few Spanish missionaries.

The rancheros liked to show off their wealth by building elaborate mansions, throwing fabulous parties, and wearing the most expensive European fashions they could afford, even when there was no one around to impress but the peones. Some of the rancheros had such delusions of wealth and power that they had their own private standing armies.

A Hard Life

For the poor tenant farmers who worked the haciendas, life was hard. Peones were not paid wages by the landowner but were assigned a plot of land on the hacienda instead. The lucky ones could produce enough food on these small plots for their families and a small surplus that could be sold in the local marketplace. But no matter how poor they were, this was the first opportunity they or their families had ever had to own even a small plot of land, and they took great pride in that ownership.

The peones who worked together on a hacienda lived together in small communities like the ones they had lived in in central and southern Mexico before they moved north. In fact, they tried to make their small towns look as much like the Mexican pueblos they had left behind as possible. There was the same cluster of poor adobe houses around a large, whitewashed church, and in front of

THE VAQUERO

The development of haciendas created a new phenomenon: the *vaquero*, the expert cattle hand who later became the model for the "cowboy" of the Southwest. Spanish missionaries taught Indians, mestizos, and Blacks to ride horses so they could look after the great herds of cattle belonging to the wealthy Spanish landowners. At first, the vaquero was simply a poor laborer on horseback, but over several decades, both his dress and his skills began to evolve into something that made him more valuable to a hacienda owner than those of just a peone. He developed roping, branding, and riding skills that were later adopted by U.S. cowboys.

The vaqueros primarily wore felt or leather hats with bandannas (forerunners of the wide-brimmed *sombrero*), cotton or wool shirts, and leather jackets with silver buttons. Their trousers were knee breeches which were often covered for even more protection with long leather leggings they strapped on called *botas*. There was no such thing as cowboy boots in those days. Unlike the landowners who wore velvet-lined leather boots, the vaquero went barefoot. He wore the spurs he needed for riding strapped right onto his bare feet.

Although the vaqueros were intelligent and practical men who were capable of learning quickly, they had to put up with relatively uncivilized living conditions on the haciendas. When tending the herds for months at a time, they slept under the stars or in crude wooden lean-tos. They built fires to cook their own meals, which usually consisted of corn mush with beef or corn mush with wild game. It was not the exciting or romantic life films and novels have often made it out to be.

the church was the same plaza where people gathered for dances and celebrations. The churches were not as splendid as those they had left behind, except for the church bells that the Catholic missionaries had brought with them on the backs of mules from central Mexico. Often the church had no seats or pews, and people had to kneel on the bare floor to pray.

As in the poorer villages in central and southern Mexico, peone homes were simply made and sparsely furnished and were usually a series of windowless rooms built around a central patio. Because there was little rain in Nuevo México, the family spent most of their time at home in the patio, where they ate, made pottery, and wove cloth.

Most peone homes had little in the way of furniture, kitchen utensils, or even basic tools. The main part of Mexico was too far away to send for supplies, so they made everything they needed themselves. Sheep's wool was plentiful, and the women spent a good deal of time spinning wool into fiber and then weaving the fiber into cloth for blankets and clothing. As more and more Mexicans and local Indians intermarried, the peasants adopted the skills and artistic designs of the Indian cultures, weaving them into their own. And as they did in the small towns they had left behind, the peones of Nuevo México celebrated religious holidays and all the major events of their lives with art, music, and extravagant fiestas.

Growing food in the arid soil of this region was often difficult, and even the rich did not have a wide variety to choose from. The rancheros lived mostly on lamb, rice, raisins, and *tamales* (steamed corn husks filled with a savory meat, vegetable, or fruit filling), while the peones made do with dried beef, *tortillas* (thin corn pancakes), beans, and chili.

At this *zócolo*, or central plaza, in San Antonio, Texas, ranchers recruited workers to harvest their crops. The zócolo was also a place to relax after a hard day's work and socialize with friends. To many Mexican Americans, the zócolo was just as important in the United States as it had been in the Mexican towns they left behind.

Nuevo México lacked other important essentials as well. There were no European-style doctors in these colonies, so the women learned to take care of the basic medical needs of their families, relying heavily on herbal remedies and spiritual cures. Formal education was just about nonexistent. What little education that did exist was religious teaching provided by Spanish priests and missionaries. Instead, sons were taught farming skills (much of which their fathers had learned from the local Indians), while daughters were trained in the art of homemaking.

A Mexican-American War Brings Major Changes

When Mexico gained its independence from Spain in 1821, differences arose between its new government and the United States over Mexican territory that included what is today the U.S. Southwest. By 1846, they were at war. Three years later, Mexico surrendered and was forced to give up over one-third of its territory to the United States, an area that included what is now Arizona, California, and New Mexico. (Texas had declared itself an independent republic before the war and shortly thereafter became a U.S. state, events that greatly angered the Mexican government and led to the outbreak of the war.) The settlers in that region who used to be Mexican citizens were now Mexican Americans. They were given a year to decide whether to go back to Mexico or to stay and become U.S. citizens. Most Mexicans stayed because the U.S. government promised to guarantee their property rights, their freedom of religion, and the right to keep their Spanish culture and language.

But the U.S. did not keep its promise to the seventy-five thousand Mexicans who chose to stay. When Anglo settlers pouring in from the East took away their land (either through fraud or by force), the U.S. government looked the other way. The few who managed to hang on to their land lost it anyway when floods and droughts destroyed their small farms in the 1880s and 1890s. The majority of Mexican Americans, now landless, were forced to take menial jobs, often working as hired hands for the new Anglo ranchers, who already looked down on Mexican Americans because of their different culture. They were barred from many restaurants, taverns, and other public places. In some areas, employers posted signs saying "Niggers and Mexicans need not apply." Those who rebelled against the prejudice and injustice were treated by local officials as lawbreakers and bandits and were often jailed or hanged. Many found conditions so intolerable that they fled back to Mexico.

Instead of giving in to Anglo prejudice, most Mexican Americans stayed and took strength in their own communities. Led by folk heros like Joaquín Murieta, they fought valiantly against Anglo injustice. They fought for the right of their children to attend Anglo schools. They refused to give up their language or religious and social customs. Many joined an underground resistance that politically opposed Anglos who were exploiting them. Some used peaceful means of resistance like underground newspapers, while others — like Murieta — became heroes by using more violent means to gain revenge. The *corridos* (folksongs) and folk legends that had been handed down from generation to generation now began to include songs and legends that were about the hardships of life in the U.S. and the exploits of their heroes. The more Mexican Americans were attacked and harassed, the more aware and proud of their heritage they became.

Mexican Americans worked backbreaking hours harvesting crops like the cotton on this Texas plantation. Because the adults' pay was so poor, children as young as seven or eight often skipped school to add to the family income.

First Immigrants: A Modern Slave Trade

Mexicans did not begin immigrating to the U.S. until 1890, when Mexican peasants were forced to migrate northward in search of work — or starve. There were many jobs for unskilled workers in the U.S. at the turn of the century — but there were also many immigrant workers from Eastern Europe and Asia to fill them. Competition for jobs was tough, which meant employers could get away with giving their workers long hours, terrible working conditions, and meager pay.

Almost all of the Mexicans who migrated to the U.S. in this period found work in one of three major industries: railroads, mining, and agriculture. Those who worked on railroad construction crews lived either in box-cars or in clusters of rough shacks near the rail lines. Miners were recruited to work long and dangerous hours in the copper and silver mines of Colorado, New Mexico, and Arizona. Both miners and railroad workers worked for very little pay and were away from their families for months and even years at a time.

Many Mexican immigrants were poor people from rural areas of Mexico, and farming was the only work they knew. They spoke little or no English, and the only work available to them was in the agricultural industry, harvesting crops. The various crops of fruits and vegetables grown throughout the Southwest ripened at different times, and the workers migrated with their families from area to area to pick them. By following the crop circuit, they could often find work all year long, but they were never in any one place long enough for their children to attend school or to live in anything but unheated, tarpaper shacks. There were jobs for migrant workers in many different parts of the U.S., but most of them migrated within California, Texas, and other parts of the Southwest.

Life in the *Barrio*

Living conditions in U.S. cities at the turn of the century were just as bad for immigrants as those on the crop-harvesting circuit. The unskilled jobs that were opening up in the textile mills, iron foundries, meatpacking plants, and garment factories paid so little that Mexican Americans could only afford to live in the worst urban slums. Working conditions were so terrible that many immigrants did not survive for more than a few years. To make matters worse, Mexican immigrants had to compete for these jobs with the masses of recent European and Asian immigrants. In the face of these harsh conditions and the increasing prejudice and discrimination they faced each day, Mexican immigrants created their own closely knit communities in the cities just as they had on haciendas and in rural farming areas. These city communities were called *barrios*. Whether they intended to make a new start in the U.S. or planned to eventually return with their families to Mexico, almost all Mexican immigrants initially found comfort and shelter in these barrios.

The barrio was a slice of Old Mexico in the middle of a hostile city. Everyone spoke Spanish, and the shops sold all the same items that could be found in Mexican markets: sombreros, serapes, handmade sandals, earthenware dishes and pottery, and all sorts of familiar Mexican food. There were even street vendors who sold the traditional street snacks of coconut candy, twists of dried meat, and roasted pumpkin seeds. Houses in barrios were usually no more than makeshift shanties constructed of plywood or sheets of rusty iron, with dirt floors and tarpaper roofs that leaked when it rained. These shanties were also usually without heat, plumbing, and electricity. Because the landlords charged outrageous rents for these shanties, sometimes two or even three families had to crowd into one house.

Those who lived in the barrio were usually desperately poor, but they all came from villages in Mexico where neighbors were friendly and always willing to help out. Those who had food shared it with those who didn't. They also celebrated together, throwing fiestas for every occasion, from religious and national holidays to marriages, birthdays, baptisms, and confirmations.

Each barrio was laid out like a small Mexican village, with a Catholic church as its religious and social center. Each neighborhood also had its plaza (usually in front of the church) where people gathered to talk, listen to music, and celebrate fiestas. As in Mexican villages, the plaza was also the main opportunity young people had to meet members of the opposite sex. Mexican parents in the barrio were very strict and did not allow teenagers to go out on American-style dates. Instead, they permitted their sons and daughters to walk (and sometimes dance) on the plaza with other people their age — while they sat on benches and watched.

Barrios were located all over the Southwest and parts of the West. Some were in larger cities like San Antonio, Denver, Phoenix, San Francisco, and Los Angeles. Others were in smaller towns or in the suburbs of metropolitan areas, but all of them were very much alike. Because of the warm weather in the Southwest, some Anglos called the barrios "sunshine slums."

Braceros, Green Card Holders, and Undocumented Workers

When jobs were scarce for Americans during the Depression in the 1930s, the U.S. government passed laws forcing thousands of Mexican immigrants (many of them already U.S. citizens) to return to Mexico. When the U.S. entered World War II in the mid-1940s, jobs opened up again, especially in agriculture and the defense industries, and Mexican labor was again in demand. At least two million Mexicans poured across the border in the mid-1940s to help fill these jobs, many of them without legal permission. The U.S. government was afraid these immigrants would overcrowd U.S. cities if they stayed in the U.S. permanently and so passed laws to restrict them. As the number of immigrants in the U.S. grew, so did Anglo American prejudice and discrimination.

The first of these laws concerned the agricultural industry and were called the Bracero Laws. These laws allowed *braceros* (Mexican migrant farm workers) to come into the U.S. — but only for the length of the crop season. When the season was over each year, they had to return to Mexico.

Other laws concerned Mexicans living in border communities. Those who wanted to work in U.S. factories across the border were issued Green Cards that allowed them to work in the U.S. during the day, provided they returned to their homes on the Mexican side of the border at night.

A large number of Mexicans chose to work as braceros or Green Card holders, but thousands more, those who wanted to stay in the U.S., entered the country illegally. Some swam across the Rio Grande at night (a practice that earned them the derogatory nickname of "wetback") or crossed the border at remote sites where there were no immigration check points. At first, U.S. border officials looked the other way. The U.S. was at war, and its farms and factories needed workers to fuel the war effort. Later, immigration officials cracked down hard on anyone caught trying to enter the U.S. illegally. Braceros and Green Card holders who broke immigration laws by staying were deported when they were caught.

Living conditions for these undocumented workers were usually terrible. Because their employers knew they wouldn't dare complain to police or other authorities, they took utmost advantage of the situation, forcing the workers to toil (sometimes at gunpoint) twelve and fourteen hours a day, seven days a week, for menial wages. Instead of even the most basic tents and blankets for shelter, they gave these farm workers plastic sheets. Some were just left to find shelter in packing crates or abandoned cars on their own. It was just as bad in cities where unscrupulous landlords financially bled tenants they knew to be undocumented workers. It was not unusual to find forty-five workers crammed into a three-bedroom apartment — with each of them paying twenty dollars a week in rent.

The Hard Fight Continues

It was not until the 1960s that Mexican American leaders like Cesar Chavez and Dolores Huerta organized national farm workers to fight for better wages and working conditions. It was a long, hard fight, with strikes that lasted years. Unions were organized in mining and other industries during the 1960s as well. The fight for civil rights, equal educational opportunities, and an end to social prejudice and job discrimination continues.

MEXICAN AMERICANS FOUGHT BRAVELY IN WORLD WAR II

Both Mexican Americans and Mexican citizens working in the U.S. joined the U.S. Army, Navy, and Marine Corps in great numbers during World War II. Many became heroes and won medals for bravery. Seventeen won Congressional Medals of Honor, the highest honor a U.S. soldier can receive.

When the war was over, many returning GIs took advantage of their GI veterans benefits to obtain home loans and to continue their education. Many left the barrios and moved with their families to other parts of the U.S., where they settled into predominantly Anglo communities.

At the same time, Mexican Americans today are fighting harder than ever to keep their cultural heritage alive. Through education, many have broken out of the cycle of poverty and lead successful lives. But while work is necessary for survival, it is not an end in itself. Neither are the material goods so many other people in today's culture value so much. Whatever their social or economic status, Mexican Americans today, as they have in the past, value family, friends, and community above all else. Whether they live in middle-class or upper-middle-class suburban communities or struggle to break out of barrio poverty, they continue to support each other with strong family and community ties. And they continue to celebrate life with their unique customs, their exuberant art and music, their passion for sports, and their ongoing contributions to all other fields of human endeavor.

Mexican Americans fought valiantly for the U.S. in both world wars. After a hard drill, this platoon relaxes with a little Tex-Mex music before shipping out to fight in Europe in 1943.

EASY TARGETS

It wasn't just unscrupulous landlords and employers who took advantage of undocumented workers. They were often swindled by racketeers who posed as lawyers promising to get them legal work permits or by forgers charging astronomical sums of money for fake documents that were not even good enough to pass inspection. Often gangs would lie in wait and rob these workers on payday. Runners would bring food to those hiding from authorities, but they would charge them two and three times the cost of the food.

A couple in their family-owned Chicago grocery market. Mexican Americans still take great pride in owning and operating community businesses, even when it means putting in long fifteen-hour days to keep them running.

CHAPTER THREE

FAMILY AND COMMUNITY
A SENSE OF BELONGING

Adriana Machuca, a fifteen-year-old girl living in Southern California with her parents, brothers, and sisters, misses the extended family they left behind in Cuernavaca, Mexico, three years ago. Aside from her grandparents, Adriana has twenty-three aunts and uncles, forty cousins, and two sets of godparents. She remembers being as close to her cousins as she is to her own brothers and sisters. She remembers a large house constantly filled with noise and laughter. Most of all, she remembers the wonderful feasts her mother and aunts prepared for all the birthdays and religious holidays the family celebrated. Her parents struggle now just to make ends meet and are lucky if they can afford to go back for a visit once a year.

Adriana's dad works in the fields, and when he can't find work harvesting, he gets construction jobs. Her mom puts in long hours in the nearby carrot cannery. Yet in spite of their tight finances, her parents always manage to send some of what they earn to poorer relatives back in Mexico.

Adriana loves the closeness of her family and knows how important it is to do things together. She and her brother and sister have always helped out in the fields and around the house, but their togetherness goes far beyond that. Whenever possible, they eat their meals, go to church, and have fun watching baseball together. One of Adriana's favorite activities is helping her dad work on the family car.

Adriana knows her parents are doing everything they can to make sure their chil-

dren finish high school and have the chance to go on to college. Her older sister Eliuth earned a scholarship to UCLA through a migrant workers program, and when she graduates next year, she will start putting some of her earnings aside to pay for Adriana's education. Adriana will do the same for her young brother, Victor. She and her two siblings also look forward to the time when they can repay their parents for all their years of hard work and sacrifice by taking care of them in their old age.

Whatever the future holds, Adriana knows she never wants to move too far away from her parents or from Eliuth and Victor. She knows there isn't anything more important in the world than her family.

Family Always Comes First

The single most important part of Mexican American society is, and has always been, the family. Friends and neighbors are important, but family, especially the nuclear family, is a Mexican American's source of strength and identity. For most Anglo Americans, nuclear family means a mother and father with their children. To Mexican Americans, it means not only one's parents, brothers, and sisters, but one's *parents'* brothers and sisters as well. Because sisters who live in the same home or same neighborhood watch each other's children, an aunt is often a child's second mother.

After the nuclear family in importance comes the extended family: both sets of grand-

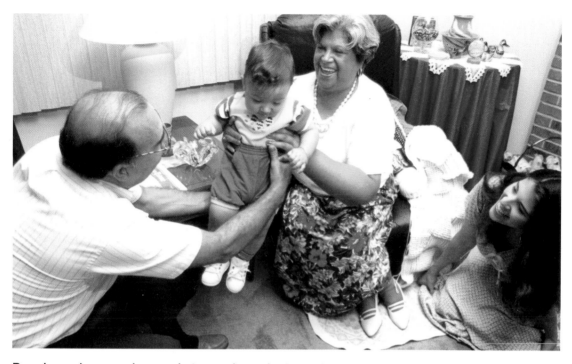

Proud grandparents dote on their grandson. In the early twentieth century, couples lived with or close to their extended families, and many relatives were on hand to enjoy (and help raise) their children. Today, Mexican Americans — like all Americans — often live far from their extended families.

parents, godparents, and first cousins (although in some families, first cousins as are close as brothers and sisters). In older generations, all these family members would often live under one roof, or at least in the same neighborhood. This is still true of recent immigrants and in many of the families struggling to get out of poorer barrio neighborhoods. It is also true of migrant families who travel across the U.S. following crop-harvesting schedules. The members of most extended families have a wide range of jobs, income levels, and lifestyles, so it is not unusual to find modern, urban family members with less affluent and very old-fashioned cousins.

In this discussion of Mexican American family and community life, it is important to note that in the 1990s, most Mexican American families live, study, work, worship, and play like any other mainstream American family. The roles and responsibilities of mothers, fathers, children, and extended family members in some of the more *traditional* families, however, still reflect the customs and beliefs of older generations.

Respect and *Machismo*

The traditional Mexican American family is founded on two basic principles: absolute respect for one's elders, and a male-dominant system called *machismo*. Under this system, the man is the absolute *jefe de la casa* (boss of the house) and his home is truly his castle. Machismo does not just mean showing respect for the male head of the household; it means obeying him unquestioningly. (If the father is dead or absent for any other reason, the oldest son assumes his role as absolute head of the household.) Husbands dominate their wives, and brothers dominate their sisters and younger brothers. It is the husband and father's responsibility to see that the house is a safe haven for his family, especially for his wife and daughters.

Under the machismo system, the traditional Mexican American wife is completely devoted to her family. She takes care of the children and manages the household, but she serves the needs of her husband first, supporting his actions both inside and outside the home. She and her daughters lead sheltered lives, rarely interacting with people who are not family members. A daughter will typically leave the shelter of her father's house only to move into her husband's.

It is important to note that the concept of *machismo* is more than what it seems to be at first glance, namely a social system based on the superiority of males. For traditional families who still operate by its values, machismo is, more than anything else, a system of pride and family respect. In the most traditional of Mexican American families, the father's primary roles have always been to protect his family from danger at all costs and to defend the family's honor. Grandfathers talk proudly of a time when machismo meant courage, responsibility, respect, and adherence to a strict code of honor.

Machismo still has that meaning to many families who are forced to live in barrio slums or to migrate for crop harvesting. These families are in more danger than most from

Traditional Mexican culture taught men that they had to be strong, tough, and strict to keep their families safe. Today, the roles of both Mexican American men and women are changing.

RITUAL KINSHIP (COMPADRAZGO)

Compadrazgo is a remarkable form of kinship based on unquestioned loyalty, affection, respect, and mutual assistance. A custom adopted from the Spanish in colonial times, compadrazgo is a pledge of friendship that must be honored above all else. *Compadres* are as close as, if not closer than, blood relatives. There are basically two types of compadrazgo: sworn best friends and appointed godparents.

When two people (usually two males) pledge this sort of friendship for each other, they feel bound to go to whatever lengths it takes to protect, honor, and defend each other. The bond is as strong (or stronger) than the bond between brothers. It would be unthinkable, for example, for a man to make advances on his compadre's wife or to do or say anything that would jeopardize his friend's standing in the community. Compadres help each other out financially and emotionally, and they would even die for one another if they felt the situation warranted it.

Godparents, the second type of compadrazgo, ensure the welfare and religious education of children and are traditionally chosen when a child is baptized. The Catholic Church introduced the social relationship of compadrazgo or godparenthood to Mexican culture, extending the sacred responsibilities of family a step further. The relationship between a child's parents and his or her godparents is very strong. When a child is baptized, its parents invite two people they like and respect to be the child's godparents, who become part of the extended family circle, showering the child with gifts and attention and playing an important part in helping the parents raise the child. It is not unusual for children to acquire two, three, or even four sets of godparents by the time they become adults. Godparents can be chosen for all sorts of events, including baptisms, confirmations, coming-of-age ceremonies, weddings, and even new-house dedications.

crime, poverty, social prejudice, and discrimination. It is easy to understand how fathers in these families still see their role as the traditional family protector: men who have to be strong — and strict — to make sure their families survive.

In most Mexican American families today, men and women contribute equally and are equally entitled to power and respect. Family roles are becoming interchangeable, and machismo is rapidly losing its meaning.

The Changing Role of Husbands and Fathers

In old-fashioned, traditional families with teenage children, the father is still the family's judge, jury, and policeman. What he says goes, and he only has to say it once. The father's role doesn't start out that way but changes as his children grow up. When his children are small, he is warm, permissive, and loving, often spending a good deal of time playing with and caring for them. Up to the time the children are eleven or twelve, it's the mother, not the father, who usually provides whatever discipline they need. When the children become teenagers, however, the father becomes very formal and aloof, even gruff. His home is no longer a place for games and laughter. Not only does he not play with his children any longer, he now sets strict rules of conduct that he expects them to obey

Today's Mexican American father shares the responsibilities of raising his young children with their mother. And he no longer has to play the role of strict disciplinarian with his teenagers.

without question. For example, he may insist that his daughter not go out on any dates unless she's accompanied by a chaperon — even when she's eighteen or nineteen years old. While he's not quite as strict with his sons, they, too, have to obey the curfews their father establishes and may only spend time with friends he approves of.

In a traditional family, the father is also allowed more independence than any other family member. He is free to come and go as he pleases, for as long as he pleases, to socialize with male friends in bars and clubs, and to generally do anything short of bringing shame onto the family name.

Of course, in less traditional families where machismo is no longer a dominating factor, the father's role has shifted. He is no longer the absolute holder of the family's power and prestige, and he now acknowledges that his wife's role is no longer limited to keeping house and having children. In most households, he no longer has total control over the family income nor feels he can come and go just as he pleases. He is also more likely to help care for the children while his wife is working and to be responsible for a share of the household chores.

The Strength of Mexican American Women

Until the mid-twentieth century, a Mexican American woman living under the traditional machismo system had basically three choices in life: She could marry, join a convent, or remain at home with her parents and take care of them until they died. She has come a long way in the last half century. The

A woman tries out a fashionable hairstyle in a shop run by this Mexican American hairdresser. Unlike traditional Mexican American women, who were expected to stay home and keep house, women today have begun to play a larger political, social, and business role in mainstream U.S. society.

ideal wife and mother was supposed to be submissive and to put the welfare of her husband and children above all else, including her own needs. She was expected to remain in the home and not interact socially with anyone but family and very close friends.

But anyone who has grown up in a Mexican American family would scoff at the idea that a woman is weak, quiet, or submissive. In reality, many poorer Mexican American women have always had to get factory or service jobs (or work alongside their husbands in the fields) to help support their families. Because of the high death rate for Mexican American migrant workers, many widows become single parents who also have kept their families going without a father figure. Many women are unmarried or divorced mothers. Even if both parents of a child are alive and married, the father may be

absent for long periods of time either following the crops (which many men do alone instead of with their families) or moving to a distant city to prepare the way for the family's arrival later. Then it is up to a woman to be both mother and father — and often act as breadwinner as well.

Mexican American women (or Chicanas, as many choose to call themselves) are proud of their heroic heritage. When Americans took over the Southwest, they wantonly violated the land rights and religious freedom that Mexican residents had been guaranteed by the U.S. government. Now landless, these Mexican were ruthlessly exploited as cheap labor for American railroad, mining, and agricultural projects, and that exploitation often included beatings and other forms of physical abuse. Chicanas were not spared that abuse. In fact, women who resisted were often hanged as examples to the rest. In spite of this, hundreds of Mexican American women over the years became heroes in their fight against prejudice and exploitation — women like Josepha of Downieville, Rosie Martinez, Teresa Unrea, and Lucy Gonzales.

Today, regardless of whether she is traditional or modern, a Mexican American wife and mother is still revered for her loving care and devotion. Often affectionately called *Mamacita*, or "little mother," she's the one who arranges all the festivities, cooks incredible and complicated dishes for all her family's celebrations, and nurtures her children through childhood. Her closest relationships are still those she has with her sisters and her daughters, and these relationships remain important throughout their lives. The bond between sisters is also strong. Daughters will go to great lengths to live near their mothers and sisters even after they're married. Couples who have had to move away for economic or other reasons return to visit as often as possible.

While devotion to family remains, in all other aspects, the Mexican American woman's roles have been changing drastically. No longer is she limited to the traditional role of having children and running a household. In fact, no longer is she expected to choose among marriage, life in a convent, and being the caretaker of her parents in their old age. Wives and mothers now not only have equal control over the family's income, they contribute a substantial part, if not all. More and more women are pursuing college educations and professional careers in business and the arts. More and more women are also actively fighting to improve their communities.

A high school baseball star in her own right, this Mexican American teenager does not know the meaning of "throwing like a girl."

A teenager's mother helps her get ready for her *quinceañera*. In traditional families, this coming-of-age ceremony can be as elaborate (and expensive) as a wedding, and the young girl's dress is often as elegant as a formal wedding gown.

Coming of Age in Mexican American Culture

Coming of age is a big event in many cultures, with ceremonies like bar and bat mitzvahs, confirmations, and coming-out parties. Mexican American culture is no exception. Among Mexican American families, the most important coming-of-age custom is the *quinceañera,* the celebration of a girl turning fifteen. A special Catholic mass marks her entrance not only into adulthood, but into the church as an adult member. (It is interesting to note that fifteenth-century Aztecs believed that a woman did not even become a human being until she was fifteen!)

A quinceañera takes months to plan, and it is not unusual for a family to spend as much on this event as they would on a wedding. In fact, a quinceañera resembles a wedding in many other ways. Typically, the girl wears a long, white, formal gown and attends a special church mass with her parents, grandparents, and godparents. Following the mass, a professional photographer arrives to take pictures. Afterwards, there's dinner, followed by a reception and dance for two or three hundred people. Usually six or seven of the girl's friends and their escorts get formally dressed up and act as the girl's "court."

Other coming-of-age customs are not so formal — or socially acceptable. Like members of the Jewish, Polish, German, and other immigrant groups before them, many Mexican American families are forced to live in poverty-ridden, high-crime urban neighborhoods. In spite of the difficult living conditions, most of these families lead hard but productive lives. They don't measure success by the size of their paychecks but by the warmth of their homes and the closeness of their families. The children of some of urban families, however, are not so lucky. For them, success is measured more by toughness and simple survival. For these *cholos* and *cholas*, the young men and women who join the many urban gangs, crime and street fights are a way of life and their way of preparing for adulthood.

Today's gangs have their own cool way of dressing, their own special slang, and even their own identifying design of tattoos. But whether they realize it or not, they are just modern versions of other immigrant gangs that sprang up in the 1940s and 1950s. They still prefer to operate at night, traffic in drugs, prostitution, and other crimes, and usually favor knives over guns because they can be more easily concealed. They are also extremely territorial and will defend their neighborhoods from other rival gangs at any cost.

Every major city and most ethnic groups (white, Black, Asian, or Latino) today has a problem with gangs, a problem that is difficult to deal with. Mexican American communities all over the country have organized action groups to offer teens alternatives to gang life. Los Angeles's TELACU (The East Los Angeles Community Union), for example, has built parks and athletic clubs, founded inner-city art projects, and orga-

A boy greets a patrolman with an enthusiastic high-five. Citizens in Mexican American communities like this one in Chicago have formed groups to protect their children from crime.

nized local businesses to provide jobs for city teenagers. A good part of their success can be attributed to the caring Mexican American parents who donate their time and effort.

Courtship and Marriage

While most contemporary Mexican Americans go about the rituals of dating, courting, and marriage in ways that are similar to those of their non-Mexican neighbors,

Everyone enjoys prom night. Today's Mexican American teenagers no longer need the traditional chaperons for school dances or other dates.

friends together and serenade the young lady — that is, sing to her from under her bedroom window. If the idea of dating the young man is acceptable to her, the young man and his friends call on the girl's parents and ask their permission for the boy to ask the girl out. And if, after a long (and usually well-chaperoned) courtship, the two decide they want to get married, the boy's father pays a visit to the girl's father and asks permission for the son and daughter to wed.

As with a quinceañera, a wedding is quite elaborate and takes a long time to plan. It is customary for the invitations to be delivered personally, when possible, and to invite all guests to bring their children. The groom is expected to pay for all of the wedding expenses except for the attire of the bridesmaids and groomsmen, who are responsible for paying for their own. The groom even gives the bride the money she needs to buy her wedding dress and the traditional rope of wax beads that is looped over the couple when they kneel before the priest.

A traditional wedding may take place over a period of three days with ceremonies and festivities that include formal confession and communion in the church, a civil wedding ceremony performed by a judge, and then an extravagant church ceremony. This is followed by an all-night party back at the girl's parent's house, where the girl's mother and sisters have been cooking for weeks to prepare all the food. (It should be noted that some couples choose to elope to avoid the incredible expense that all of this entails, and that elopement is a perfectly acceptable alternative to an elaborate wedding.)

courting and marriage customs are still very important in traditional Mexican American families. There are still some old-fashioned, strict parents who don't let their daughters out on dates unless they take a younger brother or sister with them as a chaperon, even after the daughter has become engaged. If they are children from very traditional Mexican American families like these, a boy who wants to ask a particular girl out may get a bunch of his

Changing Families

In the 1990s, the family is as important as ever. While respect for one's elders is still expected of young Mexican Americans, that respect is no longer unconditional obedience to a father's absolute and strict authority. Like other American kids, they are now encouraged to grow as individuals and begin taking responsibility for their own decisions. Women are no longer expected to stay at home and raise children, and growing numbers are enjoying equal opportunities for education and professional careers.

For almost all Mexican Americans, however, traditional or modern, the good of the family still comes before the good of any one individual, and the actions of a child still reflect back on his or her parents. As always, the family is there to provide strength and guidance. A person in need of anything from emotional support to food, shelter, and money is expected to come to his or her family first, and often a family will share money or food with other relatives even when they have barely enough to meet their own needs. On the other hand, family members who have good incomes are expected to share their good fortune with more needy family members. If a person works hard to get a college education, it is understood that he or she is doing it to benefit the whole family, not just themselves.

An individual has the total backing of his family, no matter what — unless, that is, he or she does something to bring shame and disgrace to the family. In that case, the family may sever all ties with the individual. This closeness and willingness to share are still important aspects of Mexican American family life, even when someone moves thousands of miles away from his or her nuclear family to find a better a better job, for example, or better educational opportunities. Miles may keep them physically apart, but the ties remain strong, and family members visit each other as often as possible.

Mexican American children mugging for the camera in Chicago's Grant Park.

A young woman dressed up as Mary, mother of Jesus, waits patiently for the Christmas *posada* to begin. This traditional holiday procession reenacts Mary and Joseph's search for an inn in Bethlehem the night Jesus was born.

CHAPTER FOUR

RELIGION AND CELEBRATIONS
A CELEBRATION OF FAITH

Christmas is only two weeks away, and Maria is already excited. Although only ten, she is a big help to her mother, especially in the kitchen, and today she's busy grating the lemon peel for her mother's wonderful *rosca de Reyes,* or King's Cake. The fragrant smell brings back delicious memories of Christmases past, and Maria cannot help feeling sorry for her Anglo friend Julie, whose family only celebrates on Christmas Eve and Christmas Day. For Maria's family, the fun starts nine days before Christmas and doesn't really end until Candlemas Day on February 2!

This year, her mom has sewn her the perfect shepherdess costume, and for the first time, she will be allowed to walk in some of the *posadas,* or candle-lit processions. In these processions, friends and family dress up as the Virgin Mary and Joseph and other pilgrims and walk from house to house reenacting the night of Christ's birth in Bethlehem. Maria loves the posadas. Bearing a manger and glowing candles, the pilgrims plead with the doorkeepers inside the houses to let them in. They sing choruses back and forth until finally the doors are opened and the weary pilgrims are welcomed in. This is just the prelude to a wonderful feast, or *fiesta,* and there are fiestas every night for nine days.

Just thinking of all that food makes Maria's mouth water. There will be hot *quesadillas* filled with mushrooms and cheese, tacos with spicy salsa, chicken tostadas, tamales, and so many other tasty dishes that she can't begin to remember them all. After dinner, they'll have fun breaking the *piñatas* — one for the adults and one for the children. She and her brothers have already decorated this year's clay pots with tissue paper and streamers to resemble burros, peacocks, and other animals and filled them with handfuls of candy, nuts, noisemakers, and little toys. Everyone gets to look silly taking turns being blindfolded and swatting at the suspended piñata until it's smashed open.

All this just leads up to the most special time of all: Christmas. Maria's father and brothers brought home a tree the week before, and she and her mom spent hours decorating it with colorful straw and papier-mâché ornaments. Underneath the tree they placed the *nacimiento,* or nativity scene. Compared to all the noise and fun of the days leading up to it, December 25 is a quiet day when the whole family gathers to exchange gifts and to wish each other and the world peace, happiness, and serenity. They dress up in their very best for the candlelight midnight mass on Christmas Eve and for the formal dinner her mother prepares on Christmas Day. The dining room seems almost magical, with the table set all in white, shining with crystal and

Whether the occasion is Christmas or a birthday, everyone scrambles for the treats that tumble out of the gaily decorated *piñata* when it is whacked open with a broomstick.

cakes. And there are even more holidays with special food *after* Christmas! Maria smiles to herself as she realizes how much cooking and baking all this will take. She inhales the delicious smells that already fill their warm, cozy kitchen, delighted to be a part of it.

A Deep and Unique Faith

While the majority of Mexican Americans have always been deeply religious Roman Catholics, their religious customs and traditions were not always officially recognized by the American Catholic Church. Until recently, few Mexican Americans had been ordained as priests and bishops, while few of the non-Hispanic priests felt comfortable presiding over Mexican American parishes, partly because the Catholicism Mexican Americans brought with them to the U.S. incorporated many Indian rituals and folk beliefs. As a result, Mexican American Catholics learned to depend less on clergy for leadership and guidance in their faith and more on themselves as families and communities. They view their faith as a religion of joy, a celebration of life that is not confined to church services but instead made a part of every aspect of their daily lives. It's noisy and exuberant, and the whole family enthusiastically partici-

candles and bright red poinsettias. Her mother always serves the traditional feast of walnut soup, stuffed turkey, dried fruits, and almond

A GROWING HISPANIC AMERICAN CATHOLIC POPULATION

It was not until 1984, in a Pastoral Letter drafted by U.S. Catholic bishops, that the Catholic Church in the U.S. officially recognized the importance of Hispanic Catholic Americans and the need to give them a more active voice in church leadership. This is amazing when you consider that one-quarter of the total Roman Catholic population of the U.S. is Latino, a figure that is expected to grow to one-third of the Catholic population by the year 2010. Yet even as recently as 1994, only 10 percent of all U.S. bishops and priests were Hispanic.

While most Mexican Americans are Catholic, many today have chosen other Christian faiths, including Episcopalian, Methodist, Pentacostal, and Jehovah's Witnesses, to name just a few.

pates. This interweaving of faith and everyday Mexican American culture is exactly what makes Mexican American Catholicism different than the Catholicism practiced by other American ethnic groups.

How Mexican American Catholics Practice Their Faith

Mexican American Catholics express their faith in three important ways: sacraments, devotions, and requests for protection. Sacraments are individual and family rites of passage such as baptism, first communion, and marriage. These rites include elaborate traditions and solemn church ceremonies that mark (and celebrate) the important stages of life. The church ceremonies are usually followed by large and noisy celebrations at the family's home. Although these sacraments have their basis in the Catholic faith, many of the traditions, food, dress, and music used in these celebrations have their roots in the Mayan and Toltec Indian ceremonies that flourished in Mexico before the Spanish arrived in the 1500s. Examples include the *quinceañera* ceremony that marks the passage of young girls into womanhood, special holiday tamale dishes originally baked as an offering to Indian gods, ritual offerings to the dead on All Souls' Day, and some of the music used in holiday posadas, or processions.

Devotional acts are also an important way Mexican Americans practice their faith. Acts of devotion are special prayers in conjunction with particular religious objects, such as rosaries (prayer beads) or religious medals and crosses. Most homes have a small family altar containing devotional candles, images of Christ and many Catholic saints, and other religious images, such as the symbol of a bleeding heart used to represent Christ's love for humanity.

Another important devotional image is the Virgin Mary. Shrines are erected in her

Religious candles, icons, incense, and charms are often sold at stands in city marketplaces. These religious items are used to decorate the private altars many traditional families still keep in their homes.

A young girl holds an image of the "brown-skinned Virgin," or Virgin of Guadalupe, who is for many Mexican American Catholics the most revered image of the mother of Jesus.

name for use in every type of personal prayer. These shrines can be found in fields, for example, where farmers may pray for good crops. Sometimes these shrines are even used to bless tractors or automobiles. Images of specific saints are also the recipients of special devotional prayers — saints such as San Antonio de Padua, the patron saint who helps find lost things; or San Martín de Caballero, the patron saint of the poor.

The third important aspect of worship is the request for divine protection. People seek this protection in a number of different ways: direct prayer, pilgrimages, and the use of religious objects as good-luck talismans. A pilgrimage is a journey a person makes to demonstrate his or her faith and to obtain the healing and spiritual benefits of a particular scared location, such as the Basilica of the Virgin of the Guadelupe in Mexico City or the Chimayò Sanctuary in northern Mexico. Often these places display the bones or relics of saints that are said to have miraculous healing powers.

Other, more personal religious objects are also used to obtain divine protection. These are usually things like medals, amulets, or candles that Mexican American Catholics bring to their priest to be blessed and then either wear or keep on their home altars to protect themselves and their families from harm. People also often leave offerings on church or shrine altars for the same reason. These offerings are usually left in thanks for prayers answered. When a person recovers from a serious illness, for example, it is customary to place his or her picture on the altar, along with a note of thanks. Sometimes a silver charm (*milagrito*) is included that has been fashioned in the shape of the body part that has been healed. It is common to visit a Mexican American church and see the many smaller side altars piled with these pictures, notes, and charms — tokens of gratitude for favors granted.

The events that take place in the days before Easter, including the use of religious images to depict the suffering, crucified Christ and his grieving mother, have a special intensity to them. Dressed in purple cloth and covered with thorns, Christ is portrayed as bleeding and in pain. The pre-Easter services held on Ash Wednesday, Holy Thursday, and Good Friday include vivid reenactments of the pain and suffering Christ is said to have endured on the cross. Other services are held to express sympathy not to Christ but to his grieving mother, the Virgin Mary.

Outdoor shrines called *grutas* can still be found throughout the Southwest. Decorated with flowers and images of the Virgin Mary, they are erected to give thanks for answered prayers.

THE FOLK ART OF *GRUTAS*

The folk art of *grutas* or shrines is still alive and well throughout the Southwest. These grutas (also sometimes called *niches*) are family shrines that often decorate the front yards of homes. The way they're decorated depends on particular family circumstance. For example, one family has a five-foot statue of San Martin de Porres in their front yard because he had been the oldest son's favorite saint. That son died in Vietnam. The most common reason for erecting a particular statue is to give thanks for help received or prayers answered. The most common statues are representations of the Virgin Mary — especially the Virgin of Guadalupe

and La Purisma (Our Lady of the Immaculate Conception).

The shrines are built out of plywood, cement, bricks, sheet metal, whatever is at hand — even old bathtubs. They are decorated with great care and originality, using plastic flowers, broken bits of colored glass, kewpie dolls or other dime store figures that have no particular religious significance, rosary beads, and cut flowers or potted plants. Indoor shrines are just as popular (if not just as visible) as the outdoor shrines, and often include *retablos* and *laminas* , small pieces of metal painted with the images of saints and other religious symbols.

THOSE DELICIOUS SKELETONS

What makes the attitude of many Mexicans and Mexican Americans toward death unique — especially in the U.S. Southwest — is that they are not afraid to talk about it. Instead, by mocking it, entertaining it, and making it a favorite plaything, they have learned to celebrate death as a part of life — in spite of their fears. The single most important symbol of death in Mexican American culture is an image of death borrowed from sixteenth-century Europe — a wooden figure of a skeleton seated on a throne, wearing a crown and holding a scythe and scepter. Some Mexicans and Mexican Americans embellish that image with their wonderful sense of humor and create *calaveras*, brightly painted figures with nodding heads and dangling limbs engaged in every possible human activity from dealing cards to playing baseball to blowing on a trumpet.

Around the Day of the Dead, a celebration remembering dead loved ones on All Souls' Day, stores offer skeletons of every conceivable size and material from wood, plastic, tissue paper, and papier-mâché to sugar and cookie dough. *Pan de muerto* (literally, the bread of the dead) is found in every bakery at this time. These large, round, flattish loaves of sweet bread — almost like cake — are topped with the shape of bones and decorated with purple sugar. These breads are eaten in memory of the family's dead. Spun sugar skulls are often decorated with children's names across the forehead and are given as gifts to friends in Mexican American communities. Some figures are complete skeletons; some are just grimacing skulls or bare, knobby bones. These whimsical figures are used as house, altar, and grave-site decorations as well as centerpieces, jewelry, and even hair ornaments, delighting both children and adults.

Mexican American Catholics also spend the week before Easter Sunday searching their own souls and confessing their sins. In contrast, Holy Saturday and Easter Sunday, which celebrate the resurrection of Christ and his reunion with his mother, are days of feasting and a time of joyful celebration.

The Skeleton at the Feast

Death is another important part of Mexican American life dominated by religious beliefs and rituals. While these vary from community to community, many traditional Mexican Americans, Catholic or not, believe that a person's personality continues after death in much the same way as when the person was alive. They believe, therefore, that the dead need to be buried with their personal possessions and other important objects. If the dead are shown care and respect, their souls will come back each year on All Souls' Day to visit their loved ones. It is also believed that the souls of dead people who are not shown the proper care and respect will come back to harm the living. Sometimes people are so afraid of the dead that they will perform elaborate ceremonies to keep them from returning.

When a family member dies, a large portion of the community may attend the wake, which is a social affair with food and drink. Often a friend will bring a guitar to play the dead person's favorite songs. It is traditionally the women who do the official mourning, praying to speed the soul on its way and to keep it from falling into the power of demons or supernatural animals. Some

Above: A Day of the Dead altar similar to those used by some traditional families in the Southwest. *Right:* Some of the most fun symbols of the Day of the Dead are the garishly decorated (but tasty!) sugar skulls.

people believe that the dead have to cross a river, and that a little dog swims them across. The men drink and remember the dead person with stories.

Superstition or Religious Belief?

One of the main problems the U.S. Catholic community at large has had with Mexican American Catholics is the fact that their belief system may include what many Anglos consider folklore and superstition. But who is to say what is belief and what is superstition? These are both words that refer to a faith in something that cannot be proven scientifically. We usually use the word "belief" to refer to our own spiritual or religious faith, and we use the word "superstition" to refer to the silly and illogical ideas other people have. A good example is the practice of medicine and medical remedies. Anglo American Catholics may not consider medicine a spiritual matter, but many Mexican Americans do.

Medical Beliefs and Remedies: *Curanderismo*

One area where old Indian rituals and spiritual beliefs are often stronger than the faith in Western technology is the field of medicine. For centuries, most Mexicans had a basic knowledge of herbal and home remedies for minor ailments but believed that serious illness was caused by either supernatural influences or witchcraft. Folk doctors familiar with magical healing were called *curanderos* and were often also suspected of being witches and sorcerers. In poorer villages, a person could not make a living as a full-time curandero, so he usually had another full-time job in the village, like shoe-

maker or blacksmith (or, if it was a woman, she managed a household and raised children). If villagers came to believe that the curandero was devoting too much time to black magic or had made someone ill, they immediately killed him or her.

One of the reasons *curanderismo* continues to be popular in some Mexican American communities is the fact that the curanderos not only speak the same language as their patients, they share the same economic and social status. Many Mexican Americans would have a hard time trusting an Anglo American doctor who lived in a wealthy suburb and only spoke English. They would also have a hard time affording an Anglo doctor. Curanderos, on the other hand, usually practice their medicine out of their own homes in the same communities as their patients. No appointments are necessary, no bureaucratic forms have to filled out, and no fees are charged for services rendered. (The patient is only expected to give a small donation — whatever he or she can afford and whatever is appropri-

THE NIGHT AND ITS EVILS

A old superstition that many Mexican Americans are still familiar with is that *el sereno de la noche* (night dew) is dangerous to a person's health. According to legend, there are bad spirits in the air at night that can make a person very sick, and if you plan to be outside after sunset, make sure you are well covered.

Be careful about your clothes, however, because the night dew can enter your body through your clothes as well. Don't leave your clothes hanging out on the clothesline at night, for example. People who have not paid attention to these warnings have become terribly ill and died. The only remedy

that can possibly save you if this happens is a drink made by a *curandero* from barley and arnica.

Professional curanderos operate on many different levels. While they generally concentrate on handling serious physical ailments like diabetes, asthma, heart problems, and cancer (as well as minor everyday medical complaints), they are not limited to the curing of physical ailments. Curanderos often resolve difficult social problems, such as marital conflicts, family disruptions, and disputes between business partners. They also treat psychological problems like depression.

ate to the treatment given.) Another advantage is that the patient does not need to be covered by a health insurance plan to see a curandero.

Another important characteristic of the curanderismo system is its use of natural and easily accessible medicines, such as herbs, fruits, eggs, and oils. The curandero also makes the patient's spiritual beliefs a central part of the treatment, so that in addition to being given appropriate salves and potions, the curandero's patients are encouraged to pray to certain saints and are given Catholic protection amulets to ward off evil and encourage healing.

The Folk Magic of *Brujería*

The brown-skinned, Mexican image of the Virgin Mary, known as Our Lady of Guadalupe, has become a much-revered icon of the Mexican American Catholic faith. Yet some people claim that the Guadalupe Virgin is not really Catholic at all, but an Aztec goddess in disguise. Long before the Spanish conquest, the Aztecs had honored an important goddess named Tonantzín ("Our Mother") on the very same Guadalupe site. Many archaeologists believe that the Spanish missionaries knew they could not just wipe out such an important cult, so they simply "baptized" Tonantzín and made her Catholic. As they expected, the Aztecs flocked to Guadalupe's shrines.

What the clergy did not know was that Tonantzín was not just a run-of-the mill Aztec goddess. One of her roles was "Eater of Filth," in which she helped purify humanity by accepting the confessions of her cult's priests and priestesses.

These priests and priestesses also held secret rituals to aid their followers. In other words, they were witches. And they were not

THE GUADALUPE VIRGIN

When the Spanish conquered the Aztec culture of Mexico in the 1500s, they forced the Indians to give up their traditional gods (upon penalty of death) and convert to Catholicism. In spite of that, many Indians continued to practice their beliefs in secret. Legend has it that an image of the blessed Virgin Mary of the Catholic faith appeared on a hilltop to an Indian shepherd named Juan Diego on December 12, 1531, and informed him that she wanted a church constructed on that very spot. The strange thing about the apparition was that the Virgin Mary, instead of being Anglo as she had always been represented in the Catholic faith, was distinctly brown skinned and had Aztec features. According to the legend, the local bishop was skeptical about Juan Diego's story until Juan showed him the miraculous crop of roses the Virgin had produced in the middle of winter and the portrait of herself she had imprinted on the inside of his coat.

The bishop proclaimed it a miracle and ordered that the church be built. Since that time, the brown-skinned Guadalupe Virgin has been and still is a much-revered image in both Mexican and Mexican American Catholicism and culture.

about to give up their power as witches just because the Spanish had renamed their goddess and made her look Catholic. Instead, they took their cult (called *Brujería*) underground. That cult is still going strong today, not just in Mexico, but among some Mexican Americans as well.

SANTERÍA

Mexican American culture has also been influenced by the spirituality of other Hispanic American cultures. One of the most popular has been the Santería, a religious system originating in Cuba and then brought to the United States. This magico-religious system is based on the worship of a combination of African deities (*orishas*) and Catholic saints (*santería*). Offerings and rituals, called *ebbos*, are made by initiates to the high priests, called *santeros*, who enlist the aid of these higher powers for such specific purposes as attracting love, gaining wealth, ensuring good luck, and putting a curse on one's enemies.

Brujas (as the witches call themselves) use herbs, candles, religious icons, and other magical paraphernalia to cast voodoo-like spells for their clients. These spells include love potions, good-luck talismans, fertility rituals, and spells to win the lottery, to get rid of rivals, to protect your house from burglars, to win a better job, and to counteract the evil spells of other brujas.

Although most Mexican Americans don't take Santería seriously, and younger generations may not even be aware it exists, it is still practiced in more traditional Mexican American communities. One of the main reasons for the continuing success of this cult is the same reason *curanderisimo,* the system of folk healing, remains popular: The brujas live in the same communities as their clients. They're not only neighbors but often friends. They're not only there when they're needed, but they listen to their clients' problems and sympathize with them. Where else could you get a love potion, psychotherapy, and a good cup of coffee for less than the price of a haircut?

Legends, Folklore, and Superstitions

Every culture has strange superstitions and folk wisdom handed down from generation to generation, and Mexican American culture is no exception. Here are some examples:

A pregnant woman who goes out during a full moon will have her baby born with the features of a wolf unless she carries a bunch of keys around her waist.

If you've got ants in the house and want to get rid of them, wait until the time of a full moon. Then, on three successive nights, go to the opening where you usually see them come out, take a stone, and pound on the opening, saying, "Pay the rent, pay the rent, pay the rent."

After three days (because they have no money and are ashamed) the ants will move away.

If you discover an eyelash near your eye, get it and place it between your thumb and someone else's thumb. If you make a wish while you are holding the lash this way, the wish will come true.

If you feel scared and anxious, take off all your clothes and get into bed. Cover yourself with a bed sheet and then have someone "sweep" you with a broom. In this way, your fears will be swept away.

To cure a bad stomachache, sprinkle some mashed potatoes with garlic and vinegar, wrap them up tightly in a towel, and then wrap the towel tightly across your belly button.

Mexican American children sing songs to celebrate Cinco de Mayo, an important holiday to many Mexican Americans. Cinco de Mayo means May 5, the anniversary of Mexico's 1862 victory over the French army in Puebla.

Don't walk with one shoe off and one shoe on or your mother will die a slow and painful death.

If you get your feet wet, immediately wet your head as well, to prevent illness.

Never take an old broom to a new house. You'll take all your troubles with you if you do.

Bogeyman Stories

Just as in the legends of so many other cultures, witches fly around in Mexican American legends, doing the Devil's work and generally getting into mischief. They are also frequently associated with cats. Many of these legends are told to keep young children entertained (and, of course, to keep them from doing things they're not supposed to, like wandering around outside after dark).

As in other cultures, Mexican Americans have their fables, fairy tales, and ghost legends. Ghost legends are especially popular with children. One such legend is about La Llorona, the Weeping Woman, the ghost of a woman who is said to have killed her children and then drowned herself when the children's father married someone else. When she got to heaven, the stories goes, God asked her where the souls of her children were. When she confessed, ashamed, that she did not know, he ordered her to go and find them — and to not come back until she had. It's said that her ghost still walks along streams at night, weeping and crying for her lost children.

A Joyous Faith

Whether the belief is in a holy Catholic sacrament, an herbal headache remedy, a vivid folktale, or a quaint superstition, the faith of Mexican Americans is truly one of joy, a celebration of life that is not confined to Sunday church services but that they instead make a part of every aspect of their daily lives. It's exuberant, noisy, and filled with respect and love of the human spirit.

While sugar skulls are baked to be eaten, some Day of the Dead skulls are beautiful works of art sculpted out of wood or papier-mâché, symbolizing the spiritual richness of Mexican American culture.

CHAPTER FIVE

CUSTOMS, EXPRESSIONS, AND HOSPITALITY
GRACIOUS MEXICAN AMERICAN HOSPITALITY

Elena and Pablo live in Taos, New Mexico. Their first child, Adelita, drowned when she was only four, but she is still very much a part of her parents' lives. They, like many other Mexican Americans living in the Southwest, believe that on the morning of October 31 (the eve of All Saints' Day, which precedes All Souls' Day), the souls of *los angelitos* (the little innocent ones) return to earth to reunite with their parents and feast on their favorite foods. Each year Elena and Pablo pay tribute to Adelita's spirit by decorating their household altar with flowers, ribbons, candles, and all her old toys and stuffed animals. Elena also places plates of sweet *tamales* and the *Bizcochos* cookies her daughter loved so much on the altar next to her picture.

This first day of this annual celebration of the dead is just for the children. By noon of November 2, All Souls' Day, the children's souls will have departed, and the souls of dead adults will take their turns feasting at the altars. Elena will spend the day helping her mother wash the tombstones of her father and two aunts and decorate them with food, drink, and garlands of flowers. They and other family members will picnic that afternoon on the cemetery grounds, along with hundreds of other families paying tribute to their dead friends and relatives. One might expect this to be a sad and painful day, but exactly the opposite is true. Instead, it is a joyous time filled with happy memories of departed loved ones and the pleasures of celebrating life with those who are still alive. The marketplaces overflow with bright rainbows of marigolds, calla lilies, hollyhocks, and baby's breath, and bakery windows are filled with the traditional bread and pastry of the dead and the skulls and skeletons made of candy. The Day of the Dead lets the spirits who have passed away return once more to partake of earthly pleasures. And there are few earthly pleasures more enjoyable and more satisfying to both body and soul, than Mexican American cooking.

A Rich and Spicy Cuisine

Mention Mexican food, and most Americans think of chili, tacos, burritos, jalapeño peppers, and salsa — and mostly just the plastic-wrapped, canned, or fast-food versions of these standard foods. Few have ever been exposed to the incredible variety and subtle flavoring of true Mexican cuisine. In spite of 150 years of Anglo influence, Mexican American cooking has retained most of its Mexican origins. Like Mexican cooking, many Mexican American dishes can be reduced to five basic ingredients: corn, rice, beans, meat, and chile peppers. Perhaps the most important of these is corn.

Corn Dishes

Mexican American cooking owes much of its tradition to the Aztec and Mayan cul-

Mexican food is not just tacos and burritos. Chefs throughout the U.S. create the most delicious gourmet Mexican American cuisine, from delicate *moles* to the richest, most elegant desserts.

tures that flourished in Mexico before the Spaniards arrived in the 1500s. In fact, the use of corn (or maize) can be traced back through North American history over six thousand years. Many of the names given to Mexican American corn dishes are Indian words: *tamale, pozole,* and *tortilla,* for example.

By far, the most common corn dish in Mexican American cooking is the thin, pancakelike *tortilla.* Made from ground corn, salt, and water, tortilla dough is flattened onto the bottom of a frying pan and then heated for a short time until it just starts to brown.

Tortillas should be thin, flexible, and soft. They can remain soft and warm for hours if they are stacked after cooking and wrapped in a cloth.

The uses for tortillas are almost endless. Toasted, they can be buttered and eaten like bread. Folded, they make handy scoops for bean or rice dishes. *Tacos* are tortillas that are fried in a pan until crisp, then stuffed with a filling of cooked, shredded beef or chicken, topped with lettuce, chopped tomatoes, grated cheese, and *salsa* (a hot sauce made from chile peppers). If the tortilla is kept flat after it's fried (instead of folded) and then heaped with mashed beans, meat, cheese (or whatever else your heart may desire), it's called a *tostada.* A *quesadilla* is a sort of cheese sandwich made out of two fried tortillas with melted Montery Jack cheese in between. If the corn tortilla is rolled up and then filled before it's fried, it's called a *flauta.*

Tortillas are also used to make more complicated dishes, such as *enchiladas.* First, the tortillas are softened (not fried) in hot grease and dipped in a chile sauce. They are then rolled up around a cheese and chopped onion filling and baked until the cheese is melted. A more modern version of the enchilada might be filled with shredded chicken or beef, but traditional enchiladas are meatless, which makes them popular during the pre-Easter Lenten season.

The list of uses for tortillas goes on and on. Day-old tortillas are often cut into one-inch squares and scrambled into eggs for a breakfast dish called *huevos con tortillas*. Tortilla pieces can also be deep-fried and then used to scoop up *guacamole* (mashed avocado) or a salsa dip. There's even tortilla soup!

Tamales are another popular corn dish, although they are not made from tortillas. Instead, wide corn husks are spread with *masa* (a kneaded mixture of ground corn flour and water), which is then topped with a desired filling. The tamale is then folded in half and tied with a strip of corn husk to form a little husk bag with masa and filling. The tamales are steamed for about forty-five minutes and served with some type of sauce. Just about anything can be used to make the filling: beef, chicken, fish, shrimp, fruit, egg, and even beans. Tamales can be savory main dishes or delicate, sweet deserts flavored with sugar and cinnamon. In Mexico before the European invasion, the making of tamales was a religious ritual, and the finished tamales were offered to the gods. Because many Mexican Americans still make them a part of traditional religious feasts, they've kept this spiritual connection.

Meat Dishes

A traditional meat dish that is especially popular in the Southwest is *caldillo*, a sort of

SPECIAL LENTEN DISHES

Lent, the forty-day period between Ash Wednesday and Easter Sunday, is an important time for many Mexican American Catholics. Although traditions are becoming less strict, current custom dictates that they eat only one large meal per day during this period and that they eat no meat on Fridays. (Stricter Mexican American Catholics refrain from eating meat at all during this period.)

Because Lent is so important, there is a wide variety of special foods for this season. A good example is *torta de cameròn*, a dish made of ground shrimp formed into patties and fried. The patties are then arranged in a casserole dish and baked with a sauce of dried tomatoes, green chiles, and diced potatoes. *Tortas de papas* is a puddinglike Lenten dish made from mashed potatoes formed into patties, covered with cheese, and fried. They are then covered with a mixture of garbanzo beans, orange juice, and sugar and baked until the pudding sets.

stew made from cut-up pieces of beef, potatoes, onions, and tomatoes. What sets this dish apart from the stews of other cultures are the pungent spices sweet marjoram, garlic, and cilantro. A similar dish, *picadillo*, has the same basic ingredients but adds peas, carrots, and beans.

Carnitas is a favorite pork dish made from little cubes of pork meat that are sautéed until they are tender and golden brown. Another popular pork dish is *chicharrones*, pork skins browned in a cream sauce and served with tomatoes and chiles.

Mexican American cuisine is one of this country's most popular fast foods. The ultimate finger food, the taco is as beloved (and as American) as apple pie and pizza.

MOLES

One of the most distinctive features of Mexican American cooking is mole (pronounced MOH-lay), a sauce based on ground chiles mixed with other, sometimes highly unusual ingredients. Some of the more elegant and traditional moles are made with chocolate, nuts, seeds, tomatoes, and even ground turkey. It takes superior cooking skills to create a good mole, and these sauces are said to rival those of Europe's most sophisticated chefs.

Some Mexican American meat dishes may seem exotic. *Cabrito al horno*, a great dish for neighborhood get-togethers and a favorite in the Southwest, is barbecued goat — not exactly your average American meal. *Lengua* (beef tongue) is another versatile party dish. It can be chopped up with tomatoes and jalapeño peppers to make a cold salad, boiled with potatoes and carrots to make a stew, or shredded and sauted with a chocolate and chile sauce to make a tasty *mole*. *Fajitas* are made with marinated strips of beef skirt steak sautéed with onions over a mesquite wood fire and then rolled up into flour tortillas with shredded lettuce, cheese, and tomatoes. There is also a distinctive Mexican American pork sausage called *chorizo*.

Bean Dishes

No Mexican American meal is considered complete without at least one bean dish. Most start with *frijoles* (spotted pinto beans) that are cooked in water until tender and then prepared in a number of delicious ways. *Graneados* or *enteros* are cooked whole beans eaten by themselves or with salsa. If they are added to a mixture of cooked meat, onions, and chile peppers, the beans become the popular dish *chile con carne*. If the cooked beans are mashed and then sautéed in a frying pan, they're called *refritos*, or refried beans. Another appetizing way to prepare frijoles is to serve them mixed with crumbled, fried chorizo sausage, with cheese melted over the top. This is called *frijoles con chorizo*.

Chiles

Columbus made two mistakes when he explored the Americas. He named the Native

Americans "Indians" (because he thought he was in India), and he named the chile plants he discovered "peppers" (because he thought they were plants in the peppercorn family). In both cases, he wasn't even close.

What are chiles? Technically, they're part of the *solanaceae,* or nightshade, family, which includes tomatoes, eggplants, and potatoes, but classifying them isn't quite that simple. Horticulturalists call them fruits, botanists call them berries, and the produce industry calls them vegetables. And when they are dried, they're classified as a spice. Chiles also come in a wide variety of shapes, colors, and sizes, and not all of them, by any means, can be classified as "hot."

In the U.S., chiles are grown throughout the Southwest, and Mexican American chile dishes vary from place to place depending a great deal on what type of chile is grown in a particular area. (Texans often argue, for example, over whether *chile con carne*—chile with meat — should have beans in it or not. Some even argue over whether the correct spelling of the word is *chile* or *chili.* It depends, of course, on what part of Texas you're in, and whether or not you're Mexican American.) There are plump red cherry-hots, black plum chiles, and multicolored Chinese chiles. Some grow wild; many are moneymaking harvest crops. Favorite chiles include the small, round, and very pungent *chiltepins,* the daggerlike, brilliant red peppers called *mirasols* (that grow straight up instead of hanging from the plant as most chiles do), and the *habaneros,* which start out green and then ripen to bright orange or red. (A Peruvian import called *rocoto* has earned the nickname "gringo-killer" because it's supposedly too hot for non-Hispanic palettes — but it's nowhere near as potent as the *habaneros.*) Each of these (and many others) has its own

unique taste. The experienced Mexican American cook knows just how to use them, sometimes subtly, sometimes boldly, to create the most pleasing taste combinations.

Obviously, chiles are used to spice up different kinds of Mexican American foods, but what many people don't realize is that they are often cooked up as a main or side dish on their own. *Chiles rellanos,* for example, are long, green chile peppers split lengthwise and stuffed with Monterrey or cheddar cheese,

RECIPE FOR SALSA CRUDA (COLD RED SAUCE)

Ingredients:

3 medium tomatoes, peeled and seeded

1 tablespoon parsley

2 *serrano* chiles

1 small onion

1 clove garlic

1 tablespoon (or more) salt to taste coriander

Chop the ingredients and mix them together. but don't mix too long or the sauce will become runny. It should have small chunks in it. (This is an everyday table sauce. It should be used on the day it is made and not kept overnight because it will become soggy, lose its texture, and possibly spoil.)

then rolled in flour and egg and fried on both sides until golden brown. *Chile con queso* (ground chiles mixed with cheese) is a zesty party dip often served with tostada chips as an appetizer.

Language and Social Customs

Many social customs revolve around the way people communicate, their slang, proverbs, word games, and tall tales, even their gestures and body language. Mexican American culture is rich with these types of social customs.

There is a sort of Mexican American street language, mostly used by teenagers and others who want to sound tough or "cool," that originated in the Southwest but can now be found in most parts of the U.S. This slang is commonly called *calò.* There are thousands of calò expressions, and the language is constantly changing. A sometimes derogatory calò label for an Anglo-American, for example, is *gera,* which literally means blond. Reversed comments are popular, like greeting a young man with *viejo,* a word that actually means old man, and greeting an older person with *joven,* which means young man. Di-

minutives of given names and nicknames are also common. Chuy is commonly substituted for Jesús, for example, and Lalo for Eduardo. Sometimes the suffix "ito," for boys, or "ita," for girls, is used to make a name diminutive, like Juanito for Juan or Adelita for Adela. There are also a host of slang expressions for specific situations, such as *hacerse la zorra,* to play the fox, which is used to mean skipping school.

Body language, especially folk gestures, can also be a significant way of communicating. Although Mexican American folk gestures can vary from region to region, one that is more commonly used is that of the "horns," or holding the erected forefinger and little finger, usually near the forehead, to suggest that someone is a wimp.

Every cultural group also has witty bits of folk wisdom called proverbs, and Mexican American culture has more than its share. Some examples:

En la tierra de los ciegos, el tuerto es rey: In the land of the blind, the one-eyed man is king.

El lobo pierde los dientes, más no las mientes: The wolf loses his teeth, not his nature.

A teenager strolls past a mural featuring images of Mexico's native landscape. Much of the art and vocabulary of Mexican American street life trace their origins to Mexican folk culture.

En casa del 'horcado, no se habla de cabresto: In the house of a hanged man, one doesn't speak of rope.

Es más fácil encontrar un cuervo blanco que una mujer buena: It is easier to find a white crow than a good woman.

And perhaps the best proverb of all: *En boca cerrada no entran moscas:* A closed mouth catches no flies.

Folk Games for Children and Adults

Many of the traditional games played by Mexican American children are not very different from those played in other cultures. There are action games like *El Chicotito* (Crack the Whip), a tug-of-war game called Good Angel/Bad Angel, and a Mexican American version of Blind Man's Bluff called Blind Chicken. In a version of musical chairs called *El Gato* (The Cat), the one who is "it" asks each of the others, "Do you have bread and cheese?" and while she's talking to one, the others try to change places behind her back. The first one she catches moving becomes "it." *Las Escondidas* (meaning literally "the hidden ones") is a version of Hide and Go Seek, and *La Patada del Bote* is a form of Kick the Can. There's a Kissing Tag Game that's popular with older kids, and a game called Spin the Bottle for younger kids that has nothing to do with kissing at all.

Mexican American children also like playing games with objects, such as *Canicas* (marbles) and *Oyita,* a game similar to horseshoes. They also enjoy gambling games like *Canute,* an old Navajo ceremonial game in which something is hidden in one of four moccasins and the person has to guess where it is. (This is like the old carnival shell game.)

One of the most popular games played with objects is the smashing of candy-filled piñatas at birthday and Christmas parties by blindfolded guests.

Cowboys show off their roping and riding skills in this Texas-style rodeo. Once held only in the Southwest, rodeos can now be found as far north as Minnesota and as far east as Virginia.

Adults, of course, have their own ideas of fun. Many are avid sports fans, not only following national baseball and other sports teams, but organizing their own Saturday baseball, soccer, and even (in some areas of the Southwest) Indian kickball leagues.

Raising horses and competing in rodeos have always been popular among Mexican Americans in the Southwest, but Mexican Americans in more urban areas have come up with an interesting counterpart — converting ordinary automobiles into vehicles they call "low riders." In fact, these customized cars occupy the time of hundreds, maybe even thousands, of car buffs, especially in the Dallas/Ft. Worth area and in parts of Los Angeles. It's not only a time-consuming hobby, it can be expensive — even when the car buffs do most of the body and engine repair work themselves.

The object of this extensive customization is not to get the car to run faster or to restore a vintage car to its original mint condition. On the contrary, the cars are restructured to ride so low, so close to the ground that they're usually driven at very slow speeds to avoid being wiped out by bumps and potholes. However, the cars do have to have special hydraulic lifts that can raise the chassis to legal height if necessary. By quickly alternating the lift switches, the drivers can also make their cars rear up on the back two wheels and "hop" down the street, which they often do in special neighborhood parades or in holiday or Sunday celebrations.

A typical low rider (the car, not the driver) might be a 1958 Cadillac painted candy-apple red, with a customized crushed velvet interior, a welded-chain steering wheel, a crystal chandelier, and a wine bar. Many low riders (the drivers, not the cars) have formed clubs and hold annual low-rider car shows that attract a lot of media attention. Many people also consider low riders a distinct form of Mexican American folk art.

In the next chapter we'll look at hundreds of other ways Mexican Americans are helping to form the cultural landscape of the U.S.

A "low rider" cruises slowly past spectators at a parade in Chicago. Like most low riders, this car has been customized to suit its owner, who has put most of the work into it himself.

Mexican American children carry flags in a Fourth of July parade in Boston. Mexican Americans take pride in the tremendous contributions they have made to U.S. culture — and the best is yet to come!

CHAPTER SIX

CONTRIBUTIONS TO AMERICAN CULTURE
AS "AMERICAN" AS TACOS AND CHILI

Tacos, enchiladas, burritos, chili. Camilo Perez finds it amusing that when given a choice, his non-Hispanic high school friends always want to go out for "Mexican" food. When his friends aren't munching Fritos and bean dip — or tortilla chips dripping with mouth-burning salsa — they're heading for a fast-food taco joint. (Crunching corn chips *does* seem so much more satisfying than nibbling on potato chips.) The number of Mexican restaurants in town might make sense in Dallas or Los Angeles, but in his home town of Boston, it seems amazing.

Camilo has his theories about why Mexican American food has become so popular. First of all, Americans love finger foods and spicy stews, and Mexican American cooking offers wonderful versions of both. Americans also want convenience, and satisfying food at an inexpensive price. What could be more convenient than ordering a drive-through burrito dinner or sticking a frozen tamale into a microwave and eating it six minutes later? Tortillas have become the pizzas of the nineties; Camilo figures it won't be long until restaurants are offering tortilla lasagna or mother's are fixing peanut-butter-and-jelly tortilla sandwiches for their kids.

Some of Camilo's friends love Mexican food because they're "chileheads" who live their young lives in search of the most eye-watering, mouth-searing, tongue-numbing, sweat-inducing chile dishes they can find. (They add jalapeños to everything, even their corn flakes for all he knows!)

Camilo finds it sad that most Americans never experience the rich and subtle spices used in traditional Mexican American cooking, and only taste the inevitable jalapeños or boring chili power. Even chili, the one dish that Americans think is so authentically Mexican, is nothing more than a Texas stew of sauteed beef, pinto beans, tomato sauce, and chili powder. Most of the time it's even served with soda crackers instead of tortillas — yet everyone still calls it Mexican. (Camilo loves bringing his friends home for dinner and watching their faces when they taste tamales and chicken mole the way his Mom and grandmother cook them.)

But these can't be the only reasons for the popularity of Mexican American food. Many other ethnic cultures have crunchy or spicy finger foods conveniently preserved in cans or plastic or microwavable freezer boxes. And other kinds of ethnic foods are available in drive-through restaurants along the nations' highways. Mexican American cuisine must do more than conveniently satisfy a hunger for spicy food. This is, after all, the cuisine that got its start in the mining towns, pool halls, and railroad workers' canteens as this country started its westward expansion. Camilo believes it conjures up images of the rough and ready food the settlers must have eaten out on the open range. To Camilo, its almost as if saying real Americans use *salsa* — not catsup — and that a taco is more authentically American than a hamburger or hot dog.

Resisting the Melting Pot

Unlike most ethnic groups that migrated to the U.S. in the nineteenth and twentieth centuries, Mexican Americans did not readily give up their language, religion, and other cultural traditions to assimilate into the great Anglo "melting pot." If they had, this country would have missed out on some tremendous cultural contributions. Mexican American heritage, artistry, and talent have had a lasting impact on almost very aspect of American culture, from the popular media to fine arts and everything in between, including sports, food, and rock music.

Language

Unlike Cubans, Puerto Ricans, and other Latinos, most of whom arrived in the second half of the twentieth century, the Spaniards, Indians, and mestizos that shaped Mexican and Mexican American culture have been a part of what is now the Southwest U.S. for more than five centuries. Because they were there first, they gave Spanish and Indian names to the plants, animals, and other natural phenomena that no one outside the area had ever seen before. It was only natural that the Anglo Americans who later migrated westward would adopt these existing Mexican names.

Mexican Americans also gave the Southwest its names for rivers, mountains, deserts, and lakes, as well as for towns, counties, and later, even states. *Sierra, canyon, arroyo,* and

---

SO YOU THINK THIS IS ENGLISH?

It certainly was not *Anglo* Americans who came up with words like these:

Bronco: from the Spanish word *broncus,* meaning rough and wild; this word evolved in Mexico to describe a wild horse (of which there were none back in England).

Coca: a plant whose leaves produce a narcotic; this word was brought to the Southwest by the Spanish, who changed it from the Indian word *cuca* .

Cola: a plant whose nut was said to have some of the same narcotic properties as the cuca leaf; the Spanish brought this word with them from West Africa.

Loco: a Spanish word introduced by Mexicans to describe a weed that made horses and cattle behave crazily; later also used to describe people who acted crazily.

Marijuana: a drug widely used by Mexican revolutionaries in 1910 who are said to have given it this name; "Maria Juana" is supposed to be the complete name of a *Juana,* a woman camp follower similar to a groupie.

Mosquito: a word adapted from the Spanish word mosca (for "fly") given to the blood-sucking fly Europeans first encountered in North America.

Poncho: an Indian name for a cloak the Spanish brought to the Southwest from the Arawakan Indians of the Amazon region of northern South America.

Ranch: from the Spanish word *rancho.*

Tomato: an Aztec vegetable.

MAKING A NAME FOR THEMSELVES

Mexican Americans, the second-largest minority in the United States after African Americans and the largest in the Southwest, have always had difficulty agreeing on what to call themselves. Some call themselves Americans of Hispanic Descent or Hispanos. Others use names like Mexicano, Chicano, or Latino. Here is a short guide to names often used by Mexican Americans to describe themselves and others in their communities:

Mexican American: an American of Mexican decent.

Mexicano: in the Southwest usually used to mean a Mexican, but in other areas sometimes used for a Mexican American.

Chicano: a Spanish-speaking person, usually of the Southwestern United States, who actively works to preserve the culture and ethnic identity of Mexican Americans and who actively fights for their political, economic, and educational equality; woman call themselves *Chicanas* ; the word *Chicano* is derived from *Mexicano.*

Hispano: any Spanish-speaking person, not necessarily Spanish or Mexican; also includes Mexican Americans, Cubans, Cuban-Americans, Puerto Ricans, and Central Americans; in the Southwest, it can have the more specific meaning of the direct descendent of seventeenth- or eighteenth-century Spanish colonizers.

Latino: a person of Latin American ancestry generally; includes Mexicanos, Chicanos, and other Hispanos.

La Raza: a name that is given to all the Spanish-speaking peoples of the New World, referring to them as a group with the common bonds of a spiritual, cultural, and political destiny.

montana are all Spanish words introduced into American English by Mexican Americans. So are the state names Arizona, Colorado, California, and Nevada and cities like San Diego, Los Angeles, San Luis Obispo, Monterey, Santa Anna, and Modesto all have Spanish names.

If an English-only law were passed right now that said everything in the U.S. had to have an English name, thousands of roads, rivers, mountains, cities, canyons, schools, airports, parks, colleges, states, avenues, and counties would all immediately have to be renamed. So would thousands of plants and animals. The point of all this, of course, is that bilingualism in this country is not exactly something new. Mexican Americans made their mark on American English a long time ago.

Mexican Americans in the Popular Media

Mexican Americans have done more than contribute vocabulary words to American English; they have made the Spanish language an important part of American culture. While all immigrant families speak their native tongue when they first arrive in the U.S., after two or three generations most family members only speak English. This is not true of Mexican- and other Hispanic-Americans. Instead of giving up Spanish, over 80 percent of subsequent generations continue to speak both Spanish *and* English.

Although different Latino groups speak Spanish a bit differently, Spanish is also the language they have in common with each other, making up a community that is projected to be the largest minority in the U.S. by

A DJ announces the Top Forty in Spanish. In many larger cities, more and more radio and TV includes both Spanish and English programs.

BILINGUAL RADIO

Almost every major city in the U.S. has had at least one radio station devoted to Spanish-language programming, but there is an exciting new trend that's gaining a foothold: More and more radio stations are now offering programs in a mix of Spanish and English. For example, station KSWV in Santa Fe, New Mexico (which calls itself *Que Suave* — literally, "how cool!" — and "the voice of friendship") offer news, weather, talk and information shows, as well as popular music in an English/Spanish format that is designed to meet the needs of their bicultural, bilingual Southwestern audience.

the year 2000. The Hispanic American community also represents over $171 billion in purchasing power, a fact that is making more and more national advertisers willing to sponsor Spanish-language television and radio programming, as well as Spanish newspapers and magazines.

There are currently two regular Spanish-language television networks (Telemundo and Univision) as well as two Spanish-language cable television networks (the Viva Television Network and Cable Televisión Nacional, known as CTN). While there are no strictly Mexican American networks, over 62 percent of the Hispanic community is Mexican American and much of the Spanish network programming leans toward this Mexican American audience.

Spanish language programming offers everything from public affairs programs, jazz, art and film performances (often in both English and Spanish), and talk shows to exercise shows, sports events, cartoons, soap operas, and educational spots for both children and adults. This programming does more than meet the needs of its primarily Hispanic viewing audience. It also gives the Spanish-speaking community an opportunity to introduce non-Hispanics to Hispanic culture.

Unfortunately, the opposite is true of mainstream American television. Not only does it ignore Hispanic American culture and avoid Spanish-language or bilingual programming, less than 3 percent of TV's actors and news broadcasters are Hispanic American.

Fewer still are station owners and managers or the behind-the-scenes writers, directors, and camera personnel. What's even worse is the negative stereotyping that can still be found on American television, in spite of increasingly vocal protest by the Hispanic community.

Take Mexican Americans, for example. With less than a handful of exceptions, most of the Mexican American characters portrayed on American TV are drug addicts, criminals, or hopelessly poor peasant types. If they do manage to land a more positive role, it is never as the hero of the drama, but rather as someone's sidekick or assistant. How many times have we seen a Mexican American playing the part of the hero — or a doctor, architect, artist, or any other professional for that matter?

As Hispanic-Americans who are sensitive to this negative stereotyping and who have the power to change it get more involved on both sides of the television camera, Mexican Americans will finally have the opportunity to make more substantial contributions to this medium.

The same is true of Mexican American contributions to the print media. While there are many fine Spanish-language community publications, there are few national publications like *Hispanic Magazine* that meet the cultural, economic, or political needs of Mexican Americans.

Mexican American Impact on the Arts

Mexican Americans have worked hard to preserve their Spanish and Indian cultural roots, in spite of tremendous pressures to assimilate into Anglo American culture. But not only is Mexican American culture still very much alive, it has made a major impact on mainstream American art, proving how Mexican Americans have used their rich and creative imaginations to endure.

Literature. For the past two decades, there has been an incredible outpouring of novels, short stories, and poetry by Mexican American writers. More than ever before, Americans have a chance to learn firsthand about an aspect of U.S. culture that has been ignored for too long — the Mexican American experience.

Before the 1960s, only four Mexican American writers had their short stories published in the U.S. — Christina Mena, Mario Suarez, Daniel Garza, and Américo Paredes. Unfortunately, the magazines that published their work were all little-read, scholarly publications like the *Arizona Quarterly*. Mainstream publishers wouldn't touch their work. All that changed in the 1960s when the University of California at Berkeley created two new publications solely for Mexican American authors, *El Grito* and *El Espejo/The Mirror*.

More publishing opportunities opened up for Mexican Americans in the 1970s when hundreds of small presses and magazines sprang up in the U.S. For the first time, annual literary prizes were established to honor Mexican American authors like Denise Chávez, Genaro Gonzalez, and Estela Portilla. While they were grateful for the help of the small presses that gave them their start, these authors, like writers everywhere, wanted to be recognized by the general public as well.

The 1980s and 1990s have finally started giving Mexican American writers that chance. For example, Sandra Cisnero's collection of short stories, *The House on Mango Street,* was originally published by a small press called Arte Publico in 1984. In 1991, Random House took a chance and republished the

Sandra Cisneros, a popular Mexican American author whose short fiction repeatedly makes the bestseller lists, writes about the traditions and conflicts of Hispanic American life.

Even American writers who wrote about other subjects and experiences started to incorporate some of the techniques Mexican American writers have traditionally used, like the magical realism that comes out of weaving folklore, legend, and superstition into the experiences of everyday life.

Poetry. Poetry is another part of American literature that has been influenced by Mexican American writers in many of the same ways as fiction. Like fiction writers, poets like Alberto Rios draw on the experiences of Mexican American family life, its trials, customs, conflicts, and traditions. In his successful poetry collections *Teodoro Lunn's Two Kisses*, *Whispering to Fool the Wind*, and *The Lime Orchard Woman*, Rios sets his poems in the desert landscapes of Arizona and Northern New Mexico, using magical images from Mexican American folklore mixed in with the colorful legends of Catholic saints.

Drama. Mexican American theater also rises out of neighborhood *barrio* experiences, folklore, and the religious traditions of Mexican American heritage, and its contribution to American theater has been powerful and unique.

Its roots go back to the two types of drama popular in Mexico in the 1500s: Indian plays based on Aztec religious rituals and Spanish dramas that were re-enactments of Christian Bible stories. While it may seem that the two

book — to great national acclaim. Before long, other major publishing houses began signing Mexican American writers, and national magazines like *Redbook, The New Yorker, Rolling Stone,* and *Harper's,* became eager to publish their stories. Anglo American writers like Mary Gray Hughes and Alice Marriott were also starting to publish stories about the Mexican American experience.

forms had nothing at all in common, over time they blended to produce a new dramatic form — a religious story with some pagan overtones called a *mascadera*.

When the Mexicans migrated north to settle in what is today the U.S. Southwest, they took their mascaderos with them. And, like other parts of their culture, they adapted the mascaderos to fit their new lifestyles. Eventually, they became the posadas and pastorales, the Bible stories reenacted in local schools, churches, and neighborhood fiestas on religious holidays. But a third type of mascadero, the traveling road show, had a much more colorful effect on the American Wild West. These shows, called *carpas,* were plays performed by traveling companies of professional performers who roamed from village to village throughout the Southwest. Their plays weren't religious. Instead, they poked fun at American society and politics, making their audiences aware of social problems and inspiring them to take action.

The Visual Arts. The visual arts are yet another area where Mexican Americans have gained well-deserved recognition in the past few decades. Here, too, Mexican American artists have been greatly influenced by their Spanish Catholic ancestors and by the mythology and artistry of their ancient Indian ancestors — the Toltecs, Mayans, and Aztecs.

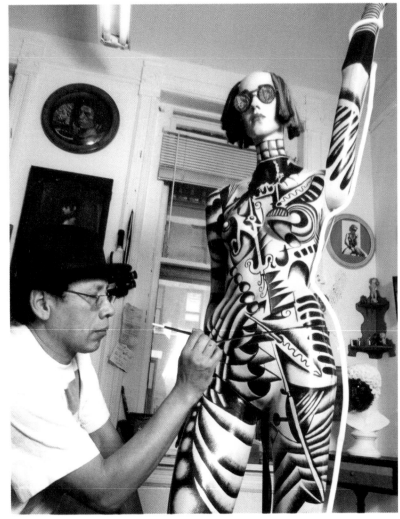

Artist Marcos Raya adds the finishing touches to his latest sculpture. Raya and many other contemporary artists follow in the tradition of Frida Kahlo, one of the great artists of this century.

An example of the Spanish influence can still be seen in the religious art form of *santos* making. *Santos* are carved and painted representations of saints and other holy figures that *santeros* (carvers of santos) have been making for the past two hundred years for church and private altars in and around New Mexico.

Another important group of Mexican American artists were the muralists of the early 1900s who were commissioned to create huge, colorful murals on the walls of public buildings. They still used many of the traditional Catholic saints and images of Indian spirituality, but they expanded their subject matter to include specifically American experiences.

Their murals became the powerful stories of the lives of Mexican Americans as migrant workers and as the unemployed who struggled to survive the Great Depression. Muralism reached its peak as a classical art form in the 1930s but has continued as a folk art form in many cities.

The sixties were an important time for Mexican American artists. Many formed collective organizations to promote their art and to help artists get the training and exposure they needed to become successful. Some important Mexican American artists include Octavio Medellín, Porfiro Salinas, Carmen Lòmas Garza, Yolanda Lòpez, Luis Jiminéz, and Edward Chávez.

Film. For many years, the stereotype of Mexican American film characters went from bad to worse. In the 1920s, before talkies, Mexican characters in U.S. movies were passionate types whose lack of control over their emotions always seemed to get them into trouble.

In the late 1920s, when movies acquired sound, the stereotypical Mexican accent turned these Latin lovers into sinister, comic, and dimwitted characters, usually a dangerous criminal or the Anglo hero's sidekick. Cantinflas, who is often called the Mexican Charlie Chaplin, is a good example of a Mexican American actor who played childlike and comic Hispanic film characters.

The Mexican Americans who became successful film actors and actresses before the 1960s almost always became successful be-

EL GATO NEGRO: A MEXICAN AMERICAN BATMAN

There is a new crime-fighting comic-book superhero on the scene. He is a mild-mannered Mexican American social worker by day who dons a catsuit at night and takes on the drug lords and "coyotes" (those who smuggle undocumented Mexican workers into the U.S.) of the Rio Grande Valley. His name is "El Gato Negro" — The Black Cat — and if he's not already on a comic-book stand near you, he soon will be.

El Gato (whose daytime name is Francisco "Pancho" Guerrero) is the brainchild of Richard Dominguez, a thirty-three-year-old artist/illustrator who came out with the inaugural issue in the fall of 1993. Unlike the violent story lines in some superhero comic books, El Gato's action scenes are less graphic. While El Gato is a martial arts expert and carries "cat's claws" to disarm criminals, he doesn't kill his enemies. Any violence is toned down. The masked crusader also wears night-vision goggles that help him track down evildoers. While the character concept of El Gato is similar to that of Batman, there is one important difference; unlike Batman's alter ego, Bruce Wayne, Guerrero is not a millionaire. Instead, he's a poorly paid, hard-working social worker who lives with his grandfather, a former wrestler. He counsels families, plays basketball with neighborhood kids, and even helps a young welfare mother carry home her groceries. Dominguez says that his comic has attracted so much attention that a Los Angeles television producer is considering adapting the comic-book hero for a cartoon series.

cause they could pass for Anglos and played only Anglo parts.

José Ferrer, John Gavin, and Anthony Quinn all had successful movie roles as European artists or statesmen. Martin Sheen and his sons, Charlie Sheen and Emilio Estevez, and Edward James Olmos are other well-known actors who play primarily non-Hispanic characters. Throughout their film careers, Rita Hayworth and Raquel Welch never appeared as Latinas. Strangely, the parts of Mexican characters in American films were almost always played by non-Hispanic actors, like Wallace Beery as Pancho Villa or Marlon Brando as Emiliano Zapata. What's even worse is that they played these characters as childlike illiterates.

Even as movies became more sophisticated, Mexican American and other Hispanic characters remained either clowns or adolescents. *La Bamba, Salsa,* and *Stand and Deliver* are good examples. Even socially conscious films like *West Side Story* and *El Norte* are about teenagers. Few Hispanic characters were depicted as complex, intelligent, adult characters.

This stereotyping did not really begin to change until the 1980s when Mexican American producers, writers, and directors started creating their own movies, like Luis Valdez's *Zoot Suit,* the Cheech and Chong movies, Moctesuma Esparza's *The Ballad of Gregorio Cortez,* and Jesús Treviño's *Seguín.* There are also a number of Chicano film festivals through the United States each year that help provide box office support for up-and-coming Mexican American filmmakers. Redonos Soto, in conjunction with Blue Pearl Productions, aired the first of a series of made-for-mainstream-TV movies on Mexican American culture in November of 1994.

Adobe and Mission Architecture

One of the most striking features of the Southwestern landscape is the adobe architecture of the Franciscan mission forts established in the seventeenth and eighteenth centuries. Because missions had to serve as fortresses as well as churches, they were made of adobe, a substance that made them strong as well as beautiful.

Adobe is the ideal building material for the climate and geography of the Southwest, and much of the distinctive architecture of this region even today is at least partly constructed with it. But it wasn't the local Indians who developed it. Before the Spanish arrived, Pueblo Indians lived in multi-story buildings either carved out of stone or built of

IT'S SAID A MEXICAN AMERICAN HOME IS NEVER FINISHED

As the family grows, it's easy to simply add on more rooms if the building material is adobe. In some places, this creates very long, one-story houses that are only one room wide. Other families prefer to build their adobe rooms around one or more enclosed patios. In either case, no two houses are ever the same. Perhaps the only feature they have in common is that the outside door never faces west — probably to keep out the heat of the setting sun. Today, however, many Mexican Americans feel that an adobe house is a symbol of low status and prefer one made of more expensive brick or wood. At the same time, wealthy Anglos in the area are consider adobe the "in" thing, and are using it to build rustic, ranchstyle, weekend homes.

tree trunks held together by dried mud. The Spanish showed them how to mix straw and dried grass with the mud, pour the mud into small rectangular forms, and then dry it in the sun. The result was a lightweight, strong, and very flexible brick that could be stacked (with mortar in between) to form even, water-tight walls. This cheap, energy-efficient, and beautiful building material is still used in the Southwest today.

Mexican American Music

Mexican American folk traditions have even found their way into many different kinds of American music: popular, country, dance music, classical, and even jazz. These musical traditions go back to the 1500s when the Spanish introduced two musical forms to the Indians they conquered: the Christian hymn and the romantic ballad.

Both of these forms went through many changes by the time they reached the American Southwest. Hymns were no longer confined to Sunday mass. Many became a sort of Bible folksong used to relate Bible stories during religious celebrations, fiestas, and parades. Mexicans also added elements of history and folk mythology to the Spanish romance form and created the *corrido*, a folk ballad that tells about the exploits of a Mexican folk hero.

Los Lobos, shown here in concert, drives home its Southwest border sound with hard-hitting rock 'n' roll. Many people know Los Lobos through the sound track of the hit movie *La Bamba*.

Corridos have been especially popular in the late nineteenth and twentieth centuries.

There are corridos about the fight for Mexican independence, about the lonely lives *vaqueros* (Mexican American cowboys) lived out on the range, about the brutality of Texas Rangers, and about the terrors of crossing the border illegally in hopes of making a better life in the U.S. Corridos were written in the sixties and seventies about Cesar Chavez and the struggles of the United Farm Workers and about Martin Luther King, Jr., and other heroic individuals who fought for justice and equality.

Another form of Mexican American folk music still thriving in the Southwest today is a lively dance music that combines corridos, country love songs, electric rock, and even German polkas. This interesting musical hybrid is known as *Tex-Mex, Tejano,* or *norteno* and is usually played by a four or five piece *conjunto* band (featuring an accom-plished accordion player) like the Grammy-winning Texas Tornados.

Mexican American musicians have achieved success in just about every other genre of American music as well. Richie Valens had a tremendous hit in the 1950s with his rock version of an old Mexican folk tune called "La Bamba." Pop singers Linda Ronstadt and Joan Baez often draw on their Mexican American roots for their ballads. Top forty artists include singers like Vicki Carr and Johnny Rodriguez, as well as popu-lar groups like Los Lobos. The members of one of the hottest rap groups of the nineties — Cypress Hill — are also mostly Mexican American.

Western classical music has its share of Mexican American artists as well, with the gifted and popular tenor Plácido Domingo and composers such as Silvestre Revuéltas and Carlos Chávez.

Plácido Domingo, one of the world's most recognized and gifted tenors, is proud of his Mexican American heritage and often performs at concerts given to benefit the Latino community.

Pitcher Fernando Valenzuela makes a putout singlehandedly by beating the runner to first. During his outstanding career with the Los Angeles Dodgers, Valenzuela was a folk hero on both sides of the U.S.-Mexican border.

Mexican American Athletes

The Grande Old Game of Beisbol. What do *un jonrón, el umpire,* and *el tres en bases* have to do with Mom, apple pie, and the American way? It's all baseball — *home run, umpire, triple* — Mexican American style. It can be said that the story of Mexican American base-ball is the history of twentieth century Mexican Americans. In spite of their love of the game, their efforts and tremendous talent went unappreciated until the last few decades.

From the 1890s to the late 1940s, African Americans and most Hispanics were prohibited from playing major league baseball in

THE KICKER IS — ZENDEJAS

Veteran NFL placekicker for both the Houston Oilers and Green Bay Packers, Tony Zendejas retired after six years and now hosts a television program in Houston called "Punto Extra" and a radio show called "The Tony Zendejas Show" on La Tremenda radio. Both shows are in Spanish and have a sports format where he reviews and previews games. During the off season, you can catch him at (where else?) Zendejas's Mexican Restaurant in San Dimas, California. Kicking seems to run in the Zendejas family. His younger brother Marty and cousins Luis and Max have all kicked for NFL teams.

the United States. One of the rules was that you had to prove you were white, so in the early days, only the lightest-skinned Mexican Americans could play. Others either played in the Negro Leagues, or went south of the border to play in the Mexican Leagues. Even after Jackie Robinson broke the color barrier in baseball in 1947, scouts for the Baltimore Orioles and Pittsburgh Pirates were still claiming that Mexican Americans were not suited as position players in the majors because of "body type and genetics." Pitchers, maybe, but that was all. Today, it would be impossible to talk about the game's most respected players without mentioning Mexican American players like pitchers Fernando Valenzuela, Teddy Higuera, and Cy Acosta, shortstops Mario Mendoza and Francisco Rodriguez, catcher Hector Torress, and third baseman Aurelio Rodriguez, to name just a few.

Other Sports. Mexican American football greats include Joe Kapp, Jim Plunkett (winner of the Heisman Trophy), Tony Zendejas, and Anthony Muñoz.

Richard "Pancho" Gonzáles, one of the most respected Mexican American tennis pros, was the winner of the U.S. Open championship in 1948 and 1949 and the Wimbledon Doubles Crown with Frank Parker in 1949. Like Lee Trevino, who won thirteen championships, Mexican Americans are also avid and talented golfers. And then there's marathon runner María Trujillo, who immigrated to California with her family in 1988 and competed for the U.S. in the 1992 Olympics. Mexican Americans are also into race car driving. California off-road race car driver Manny Esquerra is one of the hottest drivers in off-road racing history, winning thirteen major race victories in his fourteen years of driving.

Nancy Lopez, one of the greatest golfers in American history, entered the LPGA Hall of Fame in 1987. Only eleven women have achieved this honor.

A Long Tradition Continues

Almost every aspect of Mexican American culture — food, music, art, religion, dress, architecture, farming methods, even courtship rituals — has traces of both Spanish and Indian influence. Unlike most ethnic groups that migrated to the U.S. in the nineteenth and twentieth centuries, Mexican Americans did not readily give up their language, religion and other cultural traditions to assimilate into the great Anglo "melting pot," something for which all Americans should be grateful. If they had, all of us would have missed out on the tremendous contributions Mexican Americans have made to every aspect of our culture, from television to sculpture and everything in between.

CHRONOLOGY

4,000 B.C. Indians in southern New Mexico learn to raise maize (corn).

A.D. 500 A Pueblo Indian civilization, known for advances in architecture, pottery-making, clothing, religion, and government, develops in New Mexico.

1,000 The Hokokam Indians' highly developed civilization in New Mexico includes large-scale irrigation systems, stone etchings, and organized government.

1168 The Aztecs build a creative, advanced civilization held together by military might.

1519-1520 Hernán Cortés leads Spanish forces to invade and defeat the Aztecs; the Spanish introduce Christianity and the horse and marry with the Indians.

1536 Cabeza de Vaca and three other Spanish colonists become the first non-Indians to reach the Gulf of Mexico and the area that is now New Mexico and Arizona.

1539-1540 Spaniards expand into the Southwest from Mexico in an expedition led by Fray Marcos de Niza, a Franciscan monk, who is the first white man to have contact with the area's Pueblo Indians; the Spaniard Coronado, excited by tales of the Seven Cities of Gold, sets off for what is now New Mexico, Oklahoma, Kansas, Nebraska, Wyoming, Colorado, and Arizona; in 1542, he returns to Mexico without having found the famed cities; for forty years there are no further expeditions.

1582 The first of several Spanish expeditions from Mexico settle in the Rio Grande valley and New Mexico.

1769 Junípero Serra establishes the first California Indian missions, which number twenty-one by 1823 and span the coast from San Diego to San Francisco.

1810-1821 The War of Mexican Independence, which also abolishes slavery, establishes a religious monopoly for the Roman Catholic Church and ensures equal rights for mestizos and other groups in Mexico.

1823 Santa Anna establishes the Mexican Republic.

1830 Thirty thousand Anglo-Americans have accepted Mexico's invitation to colonize the Texas area, but friction develops over Mexico's right to impose such laws as the abolition of slavery.

1836 Santa Anna leads Mexican troops on an attack of the Alamo in San Antonio, killing approximately 180 men; Texas declares itself in independent republic and is recognized as such by the U.S.

1846-1848 The Mexican American War ends by the Treaty of Guadalupe Hidalgo on February 2, 1848, giving the U.S. Mexican territory north of the Rio Grande; Mexicans living in that territory have one year to become U.S. citizens or return to Mexico; the rights of those who stay are protected.

1849 California gold rush begins; Mexican American miners teach Anglo "forty-niners" about panning and mining for gold; despite this, Anglo-American miners violently persecute Mexican Americans; despite treaty guarantees, Anglo-Americans take away Mexican American land in the Southwest.

1840s-1870s Mexican Americans teach Anglos to raise sheep and cattle; the skills, language, equipment, and culture of Mexican *vaqueros* are adopted by Anglo-American cowboys.

1890s-1910 Mexicans emigrate to the U.S. for economic and political reasons; most find work in the railroad, mining, and agricultural industries.

1910-20 The Mexican Revolution causes more Mexicans to migrate to the U.S.

1914-18 Mexican Americans serve with distinction in World War I.

1920s More than five hundred thousand Mexicans enter the U.S. on visas; many more enter illegally.

1929-1941 During the Great Depression, thousands of Mexican immigrants (many of them U.S. citizens) are deported to Mexico; some of those who remain form labor unions and organize strikes.

941- 945	Mexican Americans serve with distinction in World War II (seventeen are awarded the Congressional Medal of Honor); Pachuco gangs are formed in Southwest; Zoot suit riots occur in Los Angeles; the Bracero program begins, which brings Mexican workers into the U.S. on temporary labor contracts.
950s	Many Mexican Americans move from rural communities to cities throughout the U.S.; Mexican Americans serve with distinction in the Korean War; many take advantage of the GI Bill to obtain an education and housing loans; the U.S. government launches Operation Wetback to find and deport illegal Mexican aliens; racial tensions increase and Mexican Americans feel increasingly alienated in U.S. society.
960s	Mexican Americans once again serve with distinction in the Vietnam War; Cesar Chavez starts the Farm Labor Movement; militant Mexican American organizations like the Brown Berets and the Council of Ten organize sit-ins, boycotts, and civil rights demonstrations throughout the U.S.; the Farm Labor Movement's Delano strikes against the U.S. grape industry.

GLOSSARY

Adobe	A sun-dried brick made of clay mixed with straw.
Anglo	A term that is short for Anglo-American; it is sometimes used to describe anyone who is not Mexican American.
Barrio	A Mexican American neighborhood in a city or town.
Bracero	From *brazo*, meaning "arm"; a worker brought from Mexico under a legal labor contract.
Brujería	A system of Mexican and Mexican American witchcraft.
Chicano	From the word *Mexicano*, a Mexican American who is active in keeping his or her ethnic and political identity.
Cinco de Mayo	Commemoration of the Mexican defeat of the French at Puebla, Mexico, on May 5, 1862; it is still an important Mexican American holiday.
Compadrazago	A system of Mexican and Mexican American ritual kinship, binding either two friends or a child and its godparents.
Conquistadores	Early Spanish conquerors of the New World.
Curanderismo	A system of Mexican and Mexican American folk healing.
Day of the Dead	An early November Mexican and Mexican American holiday that celebrates the return of the spirits of dead loved ones.
El Norte	The north; a term Mexicans use to refer to the United States.
Green card	Identification that proves a foreign citizen is living and working in the U.S. legally.
Gringo	A slang term used by some Mexicans and Mexican Americans to refer to Anglos.
Hacienda	A large tract of land in the Southwest, usually used to raise sheep or cattle.
Hispano	Any Spanish-speaking person in the Southwest; it can have the more specific meaning of the direct descendant of Spanish colonizers.
La raza	An ethnic term for Spanish-speaking people who share a spirit of belonging and a sense of common destiny.

La Raza Unida	"The United Race"; a political party founded in Texas in 1970.
Latino	A person of Latin American ancestry, including, among others, Mexican Americans, Puerto Ricans, and Cuban Americans.
Machismo	A male-dominated system of family order and respect, still found in very traditional Mexican American families; it is sometimes used to describe male chauvinism.
Mestizo	A person of mixed European and Indian ancestry.
Mexicano	A term used for a Mexican or a Mexican American living in the Southwest.
Migrant worker	A crop picker; someone who follows the crops as they become ready for harvest.
Mojado	Literally meaning "wet," the term refers to one who enters the U.S. illegally, theoretically by swimming across the Rio Grande River.
Pachuco	A member of a barrio gang that first surfaced in the 1940s; originally noted for wearing "zoot suits."
Peón	A worker, usually tied to working on the land.
Piñata	A papier mâché figure decorated with colorful tissue paper and filled with small toys and candy; part of a birthday game in which it is broken by a blindfolded person with a stick.
Pueblo	A township or village; also the Indian culture indigenous to the Southwest.
Ranchero	The owner of a *rancho*, a rural property where cattle is raised.
Rebozo	A long shawl or muffler worn by women, it is sometimes used to carry infants.
Santero	A carver of *santos*, or wooden statues of saints.
Tortilla	A thin, flat pancake made from corn flour.
Vaquero	A Mexican or Mexican American cowboy.

FURTHER READING

Atkin, S. Beth, *Voices from the Fields: Children of Immigrant Farm Workers and Their Stories.* Boston: Little, Brown & Company, 1993.

Augenbraum, Harold, and Ilan Stavans, eds. *Growing Up Latino: Memoirs and Stories.* Boston: Houghton Mifflin Company, 1993.

Davis, Marilyn. *Mexican Voices, American Dreams: An Oral History of Mexican Immigration to the United States.* New York: Henry Holt and Company, 1990.

Devine, Mary. *Magic from Mexico: Folk Magic, Prayers, Spells & Recipes.* St. Paul: Llewllyn Publications, 1992.

Foster, Nelson, and Linda S. Cordell, eds. *Chilies to Chocolate: Food the Americas Gave the World.* Tucson: The University of Arizona Press, 1992.

Martin, Patricia Preciado. *Songs My Mother Sang to Me: An Oral History of Mexican American Women.* Tucson: University of Arizona Press, 1992.

Morey, Janet, and Wendy Dunn. *Famous Mexican-Americans.* New York: Dutton Press, 1992.

Piri, Thomas. *Stories from El Barrio: Scenes from a NYC Youth.* New York: Knopf, 1993.

Quintana, Patricia. *Mexico's Feasts of Life.* Tulsa: Council Oak Books, 1989.

Samora, Julian, and Patricia Vandel Simon. *A History of the Mexican-American People.* Notre Dame, Indiana: Revised Edition, University of Notre Dame Press, 1993.

West, John O. *Mexican-American Folklore.* Little Rock: August House Publishers, 1988.

INDEX

34, 35; fighting against injustice, 23; and mining, 24; and pride, 23; and railroads, 24; refusal to give up customs, 23

Mexican Leagues, 75

Mexican-American War, 23

Mexicanos, 65

Mexicans: and independence from Spain, 23; and village life, 12, 13, 16; as first settlers of Southwest, 20; as immigrants, 18, 25; as labor force in the U.S., 25; as peasants, 7, 9, 10; becoming Mexican Americans, 23; perceived as inferior by Spanish, 9

Mexico City, 9, 44

Migrant workers, 18, 19, 30, 34, 70

Milagrito, 44

Milpa, 9

Minnesota, 60

Mixcoac, 10

Modesto, 65

Molcajete, 11

Monterey, 65

Mulattos, 9

Muñoz, Anthony, 75

Muralists, 69, 70

Murieta, Joaquín, 23

Music, 11

Nacimiento, 41

Nayarit, 19

Negro Leagues, 75

Nevada, 65

New Mexico, 19, 20, 22-24, 53, 66, 68, 69

Norteno. *See* Tex-Mex

Ollas, 11

Olmos, Edward James, 71

Orishas, 50

Our Lady of the Immaculate Conception. *See* Virgin Mary

Parajes, 10

Paredes, Américo, 67

Parker, Frank, 75

Pastorales, 69

Peones, 20, 21, 22

Peru (Peruvians), 57

Petate, 11

Phoenix, 25

Piñatas, 41, 42

Pittsburgh Pirates, 75

Plunkett, Jim, 75

Poetry, 68-69

Poland (Polish), 36

Portilla, Estela, 67

Posadas, 40, 41, 69

Poverty, 24, 25, 26, 27; in America, 21, 36, 37; in Mexico, 11, 13, 17

Publications, 67

Puebla, 51

Pueblo Indians, 71

Pueblos, 10, 11, 12, 21

Puerto Rico (Puerto Ricans), 64, 65

Quinn Anthony, 71

Rancherías, 10

Rancheros, 20, 21, 22

Random House, 67

Raya, Marcos, 69

Religion: Catholicism, 10, 17, 22, 25, 32, 36, 41-47, 49, 51, 55, 68-70; Episcopalian, 42; Jehovah's Witness, 42; Judaism, 36; Pentecostal, 42

Retablos, 45

Revuéltas, Silvestre, 73

Rio Grande, 26

Rios, Alberto, 68

Robinson, Jackie, 75

Rocoto, 57

Rodriguez, Aurelio, 75

Rodriguez, Francisco, 75

Rodriguez, Johnny, 73

Ronstadt, Linda, 73

Salinas, Porfiro, 70

San Antonio, 22, 25

San Antonio de Padua, 44

San Diego, 65

San Francisco, 25

San Luis Obispo, 65

San Martin de Porres, 45

San Martín De Caballero, 44

Santa Anna, 65

Santa Fe, 66

Santería, 50

Santeros, 69

Santos, 69

Schools, 10, 16, 23

Seguín, 71

Sheen, Charlie and Martin, 71

Shrines, 44, 45

Slang expressions. 58

Social customs, 58-60

Solanaceae, 57

Sombrero, 21

Soto, Redonos, 71

Southwest, 18, 19, 23-25, 34, 45-47, 57, 58, 60, 61, 64, 65, 69, 72

Spain (Spanish), 8, 9, 17, 23, 25, 32, 64, 65, 69, 71, 72; exploitation of Mexicans, 8; influence on Mexican American culture, 75; as invaders of Mexico, 10; as missionaries, 21, 23, 49

Spiritual cures, 23

Sports, 61, 73, 74, 75

Stereotypes of Mexican Americans, 67, 70, 71

Street language, 58

"Sunshine slums," 25

Suarez, Mario, 67

Superstition, 47, 48, 50

Taos, 53

Tejano. *See* Tex-Mex

TELACU (The East Los Angeles Community Union), 37

Tenant farmers, 21

Texas, 20, 22, 23, 24, 63, 73

Texas Rangers, 73

Texas Tornados, 73

Texcoztingo, 10

Tex-Mex, 73

Toltec Indians, 43

Tonantzín, 49

Torress, Hector, 75

Trevino, Lee, 73

Treviño, Jesús, 71

Trujillo, María, 75

UCLA, 29

Underground newspapers, 23

United Farm Workers union, 73

University of California at Berkeley, 67

Unrea, Teresa, 35

Valdez, Luis, 71

Valens, Richie, 73

Valenzuela, Fernando, 74, 75

Vaqueros (cowboys), 20, 21, 73

Vietnam, 45

Virgin Mary, 43, 44, 45, 49

Virgin of Guadalupe. *See* Virgin Mary

Virginia, 60

Welch, Raquel, 71

West Side Story, 71

"Wetbacks," 26

Witchcraft, 11

Women, 15, 22, 23, 31, 33, 34, 39, 46; and changing roles in American society, 31, 34, 35; and choices in life under the machismo system, 33; and household duties in Mexico, 15; and exploitation by Americans, 34, 35; and family, 31, 34, 35; and lack of social rights in Mexico, 15; as official mourners, 4

World Wars I and II, 25, 26, 27

Yucatan Peninsula, 12

Zambos, 9

Zendejas, Tony, 74, 75

Zócolo, 11, 22